*Bobby was the man [to whom] God gave the vision of FCCI.
He put together a group of men, who we now call the founders,
to look at the scriptures to see what the Bible had to say about
running a business. He wanted to learn how to integrate
his faith in business. This book tells his story of that journey.*

BILL LEONARD,
President, Wm Leonard & Co and High Tech Ministries

*At my first conference in 1994, I learned that our company exists
to honor God, create wealth for our employees and to support
Christian service to God and to people. That is now our company
mission statement. Since that time, God has led us on an incredible
journey with experiences like those reflected in this book.*

MARIAN NORONHA, President of Turbocam

*My heart breaks for the millions of people in grinding poverty
without medical care or much of anything else.
FCCI, as evidenced in this book, has the potential
to go and do business. That's what we're supposed to be doing.
It's a holy calling, and it lifts people out of poverty
into the middle class and gives people a hope and a future.*

DR. JOHN COORS, CEO of CoorsTek

A WALK IN THE MARKET

A WALK IN THE MARKET

My Story of the Fellowship of Companies for Christ International

ROBERT L. MITCHELL

MILESTONE
PUBLISHING HOUSE

Published by Milestone Publishing House, Raleigh, North Carolina.

All Scripture Quotations marked MSG are from The Message copyright © 1993, 1994, 1995, 1996,
2000, 2001, 2002 by Eugene H. Peterson.
All Scripture Quotations marked NIV are from THE HOLY BIBLE, NEW INTERNATIONAL VER-
SION®, NIV ® Copyright © 1973, 1978, 1984, 2010 by Biblica, Inc.TM Used by permission. All
rights reserved worldwide.
All Scripture quotations marked ESV are from the english standard version. © 2001 by Crossway Bibles,
a division of Good News Publishers.
All Scripture quotations marked KJV are from The King James Bible. Public Domain.
All Scripture quotations marked ASV are from NEW AMERICAN STANDARD BIBLE®. © The
Lockman Foundation 1960, 1962, 1963, 1968, 1971, 1972, 1973, 1975, 1977. Used by permission.

Library of Congress Cataloging-in-Publication Data
ISBN-10: 0615861395
ISBN-13: 978-0-615-86139-5
Printed in the USA
13 14 15 16 17 • 5 4 3 2 1

To my dear wife, Sue, who has been my constant companion on this journey, to all of the Fellowship of Companies for Christ people who have traveled with us, and to those who will travel with us in the future.

To Terence Chatmon, whose gentle pushing enabled me to write this book.

And most of all to the Lord, who took me through the battles that hindered the writing of this book. Praise be the Lord!

"The world has yet to see what God can do with and for and through and in a man who is fully and wholly consecrated to Him."
HENRY VARLEY

CONTENTS

FOREWORD

BY DR. HENRY BLACKABY

The importance of marketplace ministry is evident throughout Scripture. The marketplace is where God goes. When God is about to do something significant with his people, He raises up a spiritual statesman who will hear from Him and obey Him, and it's always in the marketplace. We're church oriented and we ought to be, but God is marketplace oriented. I believe the CEOs in the marketplace can affect the course of America.

When an executive's life is radically changed, he wants to see the lives of those around him changed also. This change affects not only the workplace but families and churches as well. The message gets spread to others, and the Great Commission is a little closer to being fulfilled.

The Fellowship of Companies for Christ International (FCCI) has stepped into the gap for these transformed executives and provides the training and fellowship they need to transform their careers into full-time ministry . . . in the workplace. They haven't put any parameters on what God is up to. I've always said the first truth of the seven realities of experiencing God is that God is always at work around you.

If you're a Christian in the marketplace, you are where you are by God's design. He has put you there. You don't work *for God*; you work *with God*. The foundational principles of FCCI found in this book will help you recognize the presence and activity of God in your business and will help you know what to do when you see Him moving. We trust the Holy Spirit to bring truth. And when the truth hits you that you are where you are, not by your ingenuity but by God's design, you'll begin to ask God's what He's up to. God brings customers to you and God brings people to you. What are you doing with what God is doing in your life? Every believer is in-dwelt by the God of the universe. And the God of the universe has something on His agenda. If He's working in your life, you'd better be careful to recognize that. Are you responding obediently to His activity? What are you seeing happen where God has placed you? He's inviting you to join Him. Are you willing to embark on that journey?

INTRODUCTION

***

Forty years ago God called me to minister in the marketplace. It happened in an extremely bad economy and I was having a crisis of belief. I had recently recommitted my life to the Lord and found myself struggling with the issue of integrity. Specifically, I was asking myself, "Do my actions reflect what I believe?" Sadly, I decided they did not. That started me on a path to be God's servant and share what I believed in the environment where He had placed me—the marketplace. It was as clear as any call to the pulpit. I knew it would be my life's work.

God used a book, a friend, and my father to confirm the call. The book was *In His Steps*, the story of an itinerant evangelist who challenges a large, social church to face every issue in life by asking the question, "What would Jesus do?" and then to act accordingly. The main storyline is about twelve people who accepted the challenge for one year. One of the people was a businessman named Milton Wright, who owned a chain of stores and tried to honor God through the business. His story captivated my heart and became foundational in building a vision in me to operate a business on biblical principles to glorify God. Essentially, my dream was to operate a business as a platform for ministry.

The friend that God brought into my life was Larry

Burkett, and he taught me two great truths. First, God owns it all (Ps. 24:1), and second, we are stewards of everything He has entrusted us with. We are to use everything we have for His glory. I read *In His Steps*, spent countless hours with Larry wrestling with these truths, and searched for a man of true integrity who walked his talk 24/7. I wanted a role model who understood that a call to be a businessman or a teacher was just as holy as a call to the pulpit, and that each of these was full-time Christian service.

I found the man I was looking for close to home… my father! It was a shocking revelation to me, because at that time I didn't know if such a man existed. My father was the same in every circumstance, consistent and God fearing. He became the model of integrity I had been searching for. The call was confirmed, and the journey that took me down the two parallel paths of faith and work ultimately became so intertwined that I couldn't tell them apart.

The work path tested the premise that you could actually run a successful business by operating on biblical principles and glorifying God. The only problem was I didn't have a business, and even if I did, I didn't know how to run it biblically. My wife Sue and I believed we were called, so we prayed for a company, and miraculously, God gave us one. It was not much of a company; in fact, it was pretty much on death's door. Of the several opportunities I had at the time, some were glamorous, even bordering on spectacular, but this one was not. It was not a good decision in the eyes of the world, but God confirmed that it was where I was to go. So, I went. I've been there ever since.

The other path was to establish a ministry. Larry and I looked all over the country to find someone who was operating a business for God's glory; one that was focused on leading employees and customers and suppliers and even competitors to Christ. And one that was building them up in the Lord, so that they might serve others and transform their companies, communities and the nation. The greater vision was that it might even be a way to complete the Great Commission. We couldn't find a company doing that. We found great Christians in business, but we didn't find anybody leveraging a business for kingdom purposes or using their business as a platform for ministry.

Larry and I were unclear about whether or not you could really operate a successful company on biblical principles in today's world, and we were also unclear on whether or not anyone else was interested in doing it. So, we decided to invite a group of committed Christian business owners to a luncheon to test this concept.

Joe Edwards and Don Patterson of Edwards Pie Company were good friends of ours and agreed to host a luncheon at their office. Larry and I invited seventy business owners; twelve came and nine agreed to meet every other week for a couple of years to study God's Word to determine if a successful business could operate on biblical principles. Seven of these men (Larry Burkett, Bert Stumberg, Bill Leonard, Jim Moye, Ben Lively, Thomas Harris, and myself) became the founders of FCC. Similar to the Apostles in Acts 4, where a group of unlearned and ignorant men did a notable miracle under the power of the Holy Spirit, this bunch of small, nondescript business owners in Atlanta, Georgia, agreed to undertake a journey to determine if God's Word could be used as the operations manual for business. Under God's guidance, we established that the purpose of the ministry was to equip and encourage Chief Executive Officers and business owners to operate their businesses and conduct their personal lives in accordance with biblical principles in pursuit of Christ's eternal objectives. The seeds of the Fellowship of Companies for Christ were planted. This book is the story of how they bloomed.

From that humble beginning, FCC was launched as a conference ministry, but small groups and materials quickly followed. Life change happens in small, transformational groups, and the materials provide transferrable concepts and guidance for companies to become kingdom class companies that truly operate with excellence. Prayer has always been foundational.

Today, the ministry is international, so we added the "*I*" and became FCCI. Technology is exploding the reach of the ministry to more than sixty countries.

This book sets forth the key concepts and principles of FCCI that have evolved over nearly forty years. They are illustrated by riveting testimonies, followed by action steps to help you implement the vision of FCCI in your business and help you on your journey through the market! This book closes with our history, structure, and strategy, presenting the future vision of FCCI. Where do we go from here?

KEY CONCEPTS

- God owns it all and you are a manager of His assets. Do a good job for Him!

- Before every major decision you face, ask, "What Would Jesus Do?" And do it!

- God uses unlearned and ignorant men, under the power of the Holy Spirit, to do notable miracles. Expect Him to use you!

THE JOURNEY

> Let every detail of your lives—words, actions,
> whatever—be done in the name of the Master,
> Jesus, thanking God the Father every step of the way.
> COLOSSIANS 3:17 MSG

Deep in our hearts, we all want to live for a bigger purpose than ourselves. We want to have something to believe in and commit ourselves to. This concept can be referred to as many different things—God's leading, our heart's desire, or conviction—but I describe it as "God's call." It is deep within us and may not be totally understood, but it is the ultimate reason for living. It is our purpose. It answers the great question of why we do what we do. When we receive God's call, the job begins, and we have to work out that call with fear and trembling (Phil. 2:12). As the great old hymn says, we must "trust and obey." If we want to please God, there is no other way. As we progress through life, we have many assignments from Him. As we prove to be trustworthy, He gives us bigger and bigger assignments, but we still have one primary call (our major assignment) in life. All of these assignments are impossible without God's enabling. We will fail in the attempt, unless we trust Him to do what He wants to do through us.

Os Guinness says, "Calling is the truth that God calls us to Himself so decisively that everything that we are, everything we do, and everything we have is invested with a special devotion and dynamism lived out as a response to His summons and service."[1]

The Apostle Paul is a great example of a believer following God's call in his career. Shortly after Christ lived on earth, Paul (known then as Saul) lived and worked in Judea, where he had a wide reputation as a high-ranking Jewish official who was working to eradicate the break-off group of Jews known as "the Way"—those who believed that Jesus Christ was the Messiah. He'd overseen the execution of many Christians, including the first known martyr, Stephen (Acts 8:1), and was proud of his work. But on the road to Damascus, where he was planning to flush out more Christian "rebels," he received God's call (Acts 9). He immediately left behind his immoral and sinful work and pursued a career that would glorify God.

Barnabas eventually brought Paul to Antioch, where he was called to go on his first missionary journey (Acts 13:2). Despite his prior status as an official, Paul willingly took the role of junior partner to Barnabas. One might have called him a "rookie." But early in that first missionary journey, he faced the devil head on and led his first convert to the Lord. He then preached the doctrine of justification by faith for the first time. Before the end of this journey, his name was changed to Paul, and he was no longer a rookie.

Paul followed this pattern for the next ten years through

1. OS Guinness, *The Call* (Nashville, TN: Word, 1998) 4.

his missionary journeys, where he wrote much of the New Testament doctrine we have today. He was fulfilling his call as he went along the way. He did it through great adversity and much fear and trembling, but God always provided what he needed to accomplish what he had been called to do. God does not do any less when He calls us today, and like Paul, we need to work out our particular call. If we want to please God, we must obey when He calls. It has not changed in two thousand years, and it will be the same in the future. It is not easy. The deeper your commitment, the harder your life becomes. To whom much is given, much is required.

All assignments and calls of God are God sized. And they are holy. They are also specific and unique. Mary was called at fifteen to be the mother of our Savior. Moses was called at eighty to lead the nation of Israel out of Egypt. Paul was in his forties when he was called to go on the missionary journeys. Calls are made to men and women of all ages, young and old. For some the call will last a lifetime. For others, it's a stage of life and then they move on to a new calling.

But for all of us, the call to honor Christ is three fold. It involves salvation, sanctification, and service. First, we are called to preach the gospel through all the earth (Acts 1:8). This is our ministry of "salvation," which is sharing the good news of the gospel of Christ, so that those in the dark will believe and see the light of Christ. Second, we are called to sanctification. Jesus, in the Great Commission, asked that we "make disciples" of all men. Once a new believer has come to a place of faith, we are to equip him or her to develop a mature relationship with God. And finally, we are called to serve. Our ministry isn't always going to be overtly evangelistic in nature, but the goodness of God is still communicated through acts of service, such as building a house, providing warm clothes for the needy, or serving food at a homeless shelter.

When we are willing to follow God's call, we will find He often expands His call beyond anything we thought or imagined. The Psalmist said, "In their hearts, humans plan their course, but the Lord establishes their steps" (Ps. 16:9 niv). We need to remember that God calls; we obey. We don't work out our great plans and take them to the Lord and ask Him to bless them. We go to the Lord and say, "Here am I, your humble servant, what would you have me do?" We don't pick our call. It's God's choice. The call is His assignment based on His perspective. He could send you into any field, and that would be holy work if it is done for His glory. The call to be a pastor (or to full- time ministry) is not a greater call than to be a teacher, businessman, or carpenter. We all have roles in the body of Christ, and they are equally important because each of us has to depend on other parts of the body to function. "We are ambassadors for Christ" (2 Cor. 5:20 ESV). Webster says an ambassador is "a diplomatic agent of highest rank accredited to a foreign government or sovereign as the resident representative of his or her own government or sovereign or appointed for a special and often temporary diplomatic assignment."[2] Essentially, we are the children of the King stationed on planet Earth for a season to represent Him and be ready for service at any time.

Our job is to bloom and flower wherever God has placed us.

2. Merrian-Webster Online, s.v. "ambassador," accessed May 11, 2013, http://www.meniam-webster.comldictionarvlambassador

Paul's plans for his missionary journeys probably didn't involve incarcerations, beatings, and other public humiliations. But his faith held firm when his plans didn't, and in Scripture we see him glory in the opportunity. We see productive ministry. We see him pray and sing praises at midnight, lead people to Christ and baptize them, and model great principles and insights for us to be effective Christians in the twenty-first century. His prison epistles (Ephesians, Philippians, and Colossians) were written in extremely difficult situations, but they have wonderful insights that can be of great help to us today when we face difficulties. Paul was so focused and committed that he was able to rejoice from his prison cell in Rome and even send us encouragement to do the same when he penned these words in his letter to the Philippians, "For me to live is Christ, and to die is gain" (Phil. 1:21).

In my case, the call was to the marketplace and was confirmed by Charles Sheldon's book, *In His Steps*. The model of integrity was walked out in front of me by my father and Larry Burkett, who was my dear friend, mentor, and the one who struggled alongside of me as we sought to see if we could really operate a company in such a way as to glorify God. The reverberating question that Larry and I were struggling with was, "What does following Jesus really mean in the context of operating a business?" It's still *the* question for Christians who find themselves running a company. The volunteers in Charles Sheldon's book who sought to answer that question pledged themselves "earnestly and honestly for an entire year, not to do anything without first asking the question, 'What would Jesus do?' And after asking that question, each one would follow Jesus exactly as he or she knows how, no matter what the result might be."[3] The motto of these volunteers would be, "What would Jesus do?" Their aim would be to act just as Jesus would if He were in their place, regardless of immediate results. In other words, they proposed to follow Jesus' steps exactly as they believed He taught His disciples to do. A newspaperman, an heiress, a social worker, and a businessman were among the volunteers who took the challenge. It was quite a challenge in 1896, and it might be an even bigger one today. Are you willing to take that challenge?

In early 1974 I had recommitted my life to Christ. That made me question and test my personal integrity. It led me to take a hard look at my life and pursue what I later came to know as a call on my life.

God had called me to the market place. I was sure of it. He had confirmed it, and I was prepared to follow Him all the way. The question, "What would Jesus do?" was daunting, but it was exciting. The only issue was that I didn't have a company to operate on biblical principles. Sue and I prayed earnestly, and God once again confirmed a path and provided me with a small business to run in my area of expertise. The owner was willing to let me run the company as a Christian company. When he asked me what that meant, I said I didn't really know but that I was working on it. I told him that I had a list of things I wanted to do that included tithing the profits, having a weekly Bible study, and putting a cross in the logo, among other things. He thought for a minute and

3. Charles Sheldon, *In His Steps*
   (Chicago: Advance Publishing Co., 1897) 17.

said that was OK, because the company wasn't making any
money at that time, so if we did make money, 90 percent
of something was better than nothing. He gave me wide
latitude on how to operate this business. God blessed it from
the beginning, which took the pressure off. In a real sense, it
was a laboratory that allowed me to experiment on different
concepts to use when trying to operate for Christ.

I was comfortable that God had called me. I felt like I
had a vision for impacting the country, and even the world,
for Christ by sowing companies that honored Him in various
communities everywhere. If you could transform communities,
I believed, you could complete the Great Commission. But
that was way out in the future. At this point I didn't even
know if you *could* operate a company for Christ, much less
how to. However, God had provided me a company I could
use to learn how to do that.

I knew that if God was going to impact the world through
the marketplace, many other CEOs and business owners would
have to embrace this vision as well. We needed companies
to sharpen each other, as iron sharpens iron, and hone the
process for teaching business leaders to use their companies
as platforms for ministry. It was very evident that this was a
God-sized vision; that would be impossible for any of us to
accomplish on our own. God had to do it. If He was going
to use us, He would have to enable, equip, and direct us. We
needed Him to bring others alongside as co-laborers and
counselors, for "Where no counsel is, the people fall: but in
the multitude of counselors, there is safety (Prov. 11:14 KJV).

Larry and I reached out to the Christian business community
to see if we could find others who would walk with us and test

this vision. We invited seventy Christian businessmen; twelve came to the meeting held at Edwards Pie Company. With this group, God provided a core of like-minded men who wanted to pursue what it meant to operate a company on biblical principles. These men would be known as the founders of the Fellowship of Companies for Christ. We were now ready to go, but we still didn't know how to accomplish our goal. We couldn't find any books or other information to guide us, so we decided to meet every other week for two years to study what the Bible has to say about operating a business as a platform for ministry. What were the principles? Did they make sense from a secular or a spiritual standpoint? Was it a wild goose chase or a call from Almighty God? Would it remain a small group or would it spread around the world? It proved to be quite an adventure. We knew that we were going down an uncharted path that was very, very different. We had to cut out a lot of underbrush. We didn't know anyone else who had ever been down that path, but we were compelled to do it. It would change all of our lives forever.

We stood at the divide and looked into the unknown. God had called and given us a glimpse of what using a business as a platform for ministry would look like, but we had no strategy yet. We didn't know where we were going, and we didn't know what to do or how to do it. But we did know that God had revealed a path to us and that we had a clear choice. We could do it our way or do it His way. We didn't know the way, so we were totally dependent on Him and had to trust Him to guide us step by step.

Before this point in our careers, the purpose of work had been to grow the business and maximize profit. Now, that had all changed. We were beginning to understand that we had a different bottom line. Matthew 6:19–33 took on new meaning for us. From now on, we would have to lay up treasure in heaven instead of hoarding money here on earth. We would be building God's kingdom instead of building our own kingdoms. If we were truly going to be men of integrity, we couldn't have one foot in the world and one foot in God's kingdom. We couldn't serve two masters; we couldn't serve God and money. We were all convinced that God's way was the best way, so we set out to "seek ye first the kingdom of God, and his righteousness; and all these things shall be added unto you" (Matt. 6:33 KJV).

In addition to the Matthew verses, God gave us many other foundational scriptures as we sought to follow Him down this path. There were many times the journey was difficult and the path unclear. We desperately wanted His direction as we began this journey, and Proverbs 3:5–6 encouraged all of us. I even made it my life verse. It says, "Trust in the Lord with all your heart and lean not on your own understanding. In all your ways acknowledge Him, and he will direct your paths" (NKJV). In addition to direction, we needed to be able to see clearly, without fog or clouds. God often gives us just enough sight to be able to take one step, and then enough for another, and so on. Psalm 119:105 speaks to that: "Thy word is a lamp unto my feet, and a light unto my path" (ASV). We clung to the Bible as our only absolute guide.

We had no concept that we were starting a movement or a ministry. We were just a bunch of small business guys trying to learn how to operate our businesses on biblical principles and honor the Lord through our businesses. This group of guys, the Founders, was in fact the first small group of FCCI, but we didn't know it at the time. We had no materials but we were meeting every other week to study the Bible to see what God had to say about various business topics—hiring, firing, debt, legal issues, paying bills, having Bible studies at our offices, tithing profits, evangelism, serving the community, and so on. We would meet and have intense discussions that some might even describe as arguments. They were sometimes heated, but we had committed to operate on the principle of unity, and God was faithful to ultimately bring us back to unity after each disagreement. We learned that making a list and checking it off is not necessarily what a God-honoring company is all about. It's more about the heart, loving your neighbor as yourself, or doing unto others as you would have them do unto you. Each company is unique and ministers in different ways. They need to work out how they believe Jesus would lead their companies. If that sounds difficult, it is. The good news for you is that FCCI has thirty-five years of developing materials and study guides to help people just like you to implement this vision in your company. This book will highlight many of those principles and give practical takeaways to apply.

Small groups are at the heart of the "how." Practical biblical business teaching is foundational, but our relationships are built for a lifetime. What we learned in those early days was that life change happens in small groups. We learned the value of friendships, sharing confidential details of our lives, being held accountable, and studying together to achieve a common purpose. In a word, we bonded together on a deep and intimate basis. This is what happens in small groups, and over the years we've seen it happen in literally hundreds of groups around the world. *We all desperately need it!* It is lonely at the top of our organizations, and it is essential that we have a way to discuss difficult issues that are inappropriate to share within our own chain of command. It is essential that we can draw on godly wisdom in total security from people who have our best interests at heart. The relationships developed in FCCI small groups are forever.

Our little group met for two more years, and then we decided to share what we had learned with others. We decided to host a conference in early 1980 and to establish a conference ministry. We were at the point where we needed an official name. We had called our small group Christian Business Fellowship, but as we discussed the name of the new ministry, we had some pushback. Several people objected to the term "Christian business," because a business cannot accept Christ and therefore cannot be Christian. We prayed for unity about the name. Everyone agreed that we were companies for Christ, and we all liked *fellowship* because that indicated that we were an intimate, like-minded community. So the name Fellowship of Companies for Christ was born out of prayer and a desire for unity.

We modeled the ministry after a trade association that Bert Stumberg had been a member of. We planned to have three conferences a year—a one-day conference, a two-day conference, and a three-day conference. The one- and two-day conferences were to be on practical, nitty-gritty applications in a reachable city (Atlanta), and the three-day conference was to be focused on spiritual truth at a resort location. They were immediate successes. The message of using a business as a platform for ministry resonated with the people. They were eager to use what God had entrusted them with (their businesses) for His glory. But they wanted more. A common question was, "What do we do between the meetings?" We quickly realized that we needed to add local fellowship groups and to provide teaching materials. That was a big task for a bunch of small business owners who were volunteers for this work with no ministry resources, staff, or knowledge of how to run a ministry in addition to the full-time job of running their own companies! But God was good, and He met our needs again. The ministry went forward with conferences, groups, and materials, all undergirded with much prayer. God blessed it and much fruit has been the result.

Key Concepts

- "The world is yet to see what God can do with and for and through and in a man who is fully and wholly consecrated to Him." – Henry Varley

- God still calls people today, and when He calls us, He equips us.

- It's lonely at the top, and we all desperately need the fellowship of a small group.

- If you are running a company for Christ, your bottom line has to reflect that you are different, not better.

BRUCE WILKINSON
Calling and Vocation

Getting involved in marketplace ministry wasn't on my to-do list! I'm a seminary graduate, so I was ill prepared to talk about anything outside of church. You know seminary is a wonderful place, but nobody who is a professor there has been in business. They've all been in ministry or academia. So [the leaders of FCCI] came to a number of my classes, then they came over to my office one day and asked me to speak to them about how to use the Bible in business. I told them I wasn't prepared to do that. The answer was, "No, thank you." They were very kind and left, but a few weeks later they called and came again a second time.

I said, "Listen, I don't . . . I hardly even know what a balance sheet is, let alone how to run a business from God's point of view." So I turned them down. I didn't think I'd hear from them again, but Bert and Bobby came back a third time and said they weren't leaving the office until I said yes. Bert Stumberg was one of my heroes, and well, he meant it. I caved. Not because I wanted to do it or felt like I was prepared, but simply because they were so persuasive, I said OK. I remember thinking to myself, *Well, I'll just go get a bunch of books on this stuff and learn the material and then come back and put it together as best as I can.* I went out to the bookstores and Christian libraries and was dumbfounded. There was only one book—*one*—that I could find back then that had anything to do with this topic. I mean there were books on ethics but not on business. It was written by Stanley Tam, *God Owns My*

Business. It's a great book.

So I hit a panic button. I had agreed to go speak for a number of days but had no content and no idea what to do. It's like a blank slate. I would be talking about something I'd not heard other people talk about; I'd not read much about [the subject], so I was just driven back to Scripture and started hunting from scratch. I spent a lot of time in preparation and seeking and trying to unravel the answer to the question, "How do you run a business for Christ?" The Bible is full of answers as long as you have the right question and you're diligent enough in seeking God's will. You just have to open your eyes to see what's in print and then to try and put it together in a way that makes sense to the people to whom you're speaking.

It was a life-changing first event down at Point Clear, Alabama, in the early days. God just showed up. Oftentimes, when God launches something, He'll give you a number of "burning bush" experiences to look back on when you go through trials and testing so you know for sure that God was in it because of events that occurred. And that conference turned out to be a burning bush for us. Everybody was so touched and encouraged that they wanted to do another one. I couldn't believe they were saying this! We went away again six weeks later. I had prepared all new material, and that was the foundation upon which we began to form the culture, the values, the belief, the vision, the standards, the affirmations of what today has become the foundation of FCC.

Then we (Bert Stumberg, Bobby Mitchell, Bill Leonard, Jim Moye, Smith Lanier, Ben Lively, Thomas Harris, Jimmy Pursell, and a couple other guys) began to meet. For board meetings we'd go down to Bert's house on the lake in Alabama for a weekend. We'd have so much fellowship and discussion that it became obvious that we were on to something. It was meeting our needs, and we figured it would meet other people's needs as well. We invited some other people just to see what would happen, and God just opened the doors.

For many years there wasn't much talk in the secular marketplace about your character, your personal life. There was a big divorce between those two parts of your life. Eventually Stephen Covey came out with his book [*Seven Habits of Highly Effective People*], and other people came out with books about character, but Jesus built his whole ministry on helping a handful of businessmen and teaching them about character. So we said that is the basis—it's who we are.

Your business is a platform, like a stage. You have lots of roles in life—be it a husband, or a father, or a businessman. How you play your role, how you live out your life on that platform, is probably the greatest opportunity you have to affect people for Christ and for the kingdom. In the early days, I'd teach about this idea. I'd ask, "What is your profession?" Most people think, *builder, marketer, engineer*, and so on. But the word *profession* comes from the root word "to profess." In the olden days, they saw your life's profession as the place from which you are able to profess Christ. We've lost our roots.

We have lost the concept that our vocation is a calling from God. The calling from God *may* be to pastor a church, but God calls less than one percent of Christians to the pastor's platform. But I would say 99 percent of all the people that come to me for counsel say their pastors, though well meaning, never speak to where they live as businessmen. It's not because pastors want to be irrelevant about that part of life, but for the most part, pastors haven't been in a profession outside the ministry. They've not wrestled with profit. They've not wrestled with competition. They've not wrestled with marketing issues and cash flow pressures and all the rest. Therefore, they don't [speak on this topic], just as I didn't. But the truth is 95 percent of the people I face when I speak in a church live on the platform called "the marketplace." If anything, I'd better be speaking to them about where they live. God has called them into the marketplace just as much as He's called me to the pulpit.

FCCI

CHAPTER 2

YOU ARE A STEWARD

Commit your work to the Lord,
and your plans will be established.

PROVERBS 16:3 ESV

One of the foundational principles of FCCI is that God owns it all, and we are stewards of what He has entrusted us with. We are to use our earthly resources for His glory, not ours. This is *stewardship*.

Many Christians do not have an accurate concept of what stewardship is all about. When we hear the word *stewardship*, most of us think about the program at church where we are asked to increase our contributions to the budget. Unfortunately, that is a very narrow view. In his book, *The Steward*, John Haggai expands on Dr. Han Kyung Chik's definition of *stewardship* as being "the practice of systematic and proportionate giving of time, abilities, material possessions . . . *and all God's gifts to us* . . . based on the conviction that these are a trust from God, to be used in His service, for the benefit of all mankind in grateful acknowledgement of Christ's redeeming love."[4] Essentially, we are managers of

4. John Haggai, *The Steward* (Atlanta: The Haggai Institute, 1983) 9.

God's "stuff"—all of His assets, not just finances.

The steward or manager of a business has to manage every facet of the business. In a typical manufacturing company, the General Manager has to manage raw materials, people, utilities, tooling, repairs, supplies, insurance, interest, investments and a number of other items. He has to control the cost in each area and optimize the profit. Different types of companies have to manage different line items, but essentially all secular companies are seeking, driving, and focusing on making the most profit possible. Sometimes companies push the limits of the law, and sometimes they operate with great integrity. However, running a company for Christ is very different. There is a different bottom line. Secular business management is based on growth for profit's sake, but Christ has called us to a more far-reaching purpose. The bar is high. What would Jesus do? The steward has to consider that in every area. The process of running a business biblically can be the most important product you turn out; to those watching you, the process is the product.

All companies must make a profit or they will not be able to stay in business, and they certainly will not be able to grow. Profit is good and necessary, but there is more to the bottom line of a company operating on biblical principles than profit. In the last chapter, we touched on the three S's of FCCI: salvation, sanctification, and service. These three themes run throughout the Bible, and the steward that is running a company for Christ will have to incorporate them into his business plan and have goals for each one.

SALVATION

A typical company of one hundred employees has ten thousand opportunities to impact people for the kingdom every year. That includes suppliers, customers, competitors, truck drivers, and any other business contact. Most of us don't even think about these relationships, but Peter tells us to, "Always be prepared to give an answer to everyone who asks you to give the reason for the hope you have" (1 Pet. 3:15 NIV). We must be intentional in *all* our relationships, not just those in our personal lives. Defending the gospel with love and respect needs to be the habit of our lives.

This idea arose years ago at an FCCI meeting in Atlanta where Bruce Wilkinson, formerly president of Walk Thru the Bible, was teaching on Salvation, Sanctification, and Service. He encouraged us to focus on leading more people to Christ through our companies than we had the previous year. "If you led ten people to the Lord last year," he asked, "could you lead twelve or fifteen to the Lord this year?" Then, suddenly, he stopped. He was thoughtful for a few seconds then said it had just occurred to him that Walk Thru was not focused on leading people to Christ, even though it was a great ministry for discipleship. In those days, they were teaching 7,500 seminars per year, but those seminars did not include a basic explanation of the gospel geared toward unbelievers. They were missing a great evangelism opportunity, and it was right in front of their eyes! On stage he promised that from that moment on, Walk Thru the Bible would clearly share the gospel at every seminar they taught.

The following year Bruce reported the results of this change in their operating policy. Walk Thru the Bible was averaging 50,000 salvations per year! What a fantastic "bottom line". The return on investment was extraordinary, and it all flowed from the intentionality of implementing that truth that we must *always* be ready to share the gospel. What opportunities for evangelism are you missing in the everyday activities of your business?

SANCTIFICATION

Sanctification is a long unusual word that means "set apart for God." It can also mean to grow someone up in the Lord and equip them for the work of the ministry, or simply to disciple them. When someone is led to the Lord through your company, you have a responsibility to nurture them so they can grow in their faith. Obviously, your role in their discipleship depends on your access to the person and where they live.

At FCCI, we initially try to plug them into a local church. If they live out of town, we network with FCCI people in other cities to find several good churches near where they live. If they work at our company, we encourage them to come to the company Bible study. If they don't have a good church home and they are particularly hungry, we may assign one of our more mature employees to take them through a discipleship course. If they have a particular need (such as finance, marriage, parenting, etc.), we might send them to a course at our expense. If we see what we consider to be a serious problem, such as a possible marital breakup, we might provide a counselor or send them out for a weekend retreat specializing in putting marriages back together.

It is important for the manager or CEO to understand his or her role as a shepherd. You have a responsibility to tend your sheep, but all companies are unique, and you will have to develop methods to fit your particular business. Of course, there are many legal restrictions that any executive should be aware of, but FCCI members clearly communicate to their employees that all outreach opportunities are completely voluntary and will have no impact on their professional careers. One of the great benefits of being in a fellowship is that we can share best practices and receive godly wisdom and advice from someone who is further down life's path than we are.

SERVICE

The nature of service is that we help others in our companies, neighborhoods, communities, and beyond without any hope of gain. Acts of service aren't overtly "spiritual." It's simply using our time, abilities, and material possessions to help others.

The parable of the Good Samaritan in Luke 10:30-37 gives us a vivid example of service. Jesus told the story of a man traveling from Jerusalem to Jericho, who was attacked, stripped, and left for dead. Not long after, a priest came down the same road, saw the injured man but passed by on the other side of the road. A Levite also came down that road, saw the man and passed by on the other side. But when a Samaritan came down that road, he saw the man and *had compassion on him.* He treated and bound his wounds and took him to an inn. He paid the innkeeper to take care of him and said he would also cover any additional charges. Jesus then asked which of the three men was a neighbor to the beaten man. The answer was the one who showed mercy on him. Jesus finished the parable by saying to all of us through the ages, *"Go and do likewise."* This Samaritan man helped his enemy (a Jew) and not only didn't get a reward,, but he gave a considerable amount of his own money to help him get well.

We need to serve with the same amount of compassion. Sometimes we need to help a person like the Good Samaritan did. At other times the call of service can require many people and result in significant transformation of whole communities. When God invites you to join in serving others, it is a God-sized project whether we see it as large or small.

Many times during my business career, employees have asked for a little help. It has always been awkward, because we were often short on money or couldn't necessarily do the same thing for all employees who needed it. We looked for a solution to take the burden off of the company, and yet, meet the needs of our employees and involve more people in the process. So several years ago, we decided to start a benevolence fund for no other purpose than to help our employees in need. Our company gave the seed money, and we opened it up to all of our employees to contribute. An employee committee was selected to review requests and decide how much money to give out. A third-party, non-profit organization, Helping Hands Ministries in Tallulah Falls, Georgia, holds the funds and distributes the money. It's a wonderful joint effort by our employees and Helping Hands and is self-perpetuating.

There are many other projects we've participated in over the years like helping fire-ravaged families to rebuild or collecting food and toys for poor families and delivering them at Christmas. When the Olympics came to Atlanta in 1996, we joined with a number of other companies to do an urban renewal project next to Olympic stadium. We greatly improved the city's appearance by building condos that were used during the Olympics and then sold after the games to worthy inner city employees at significantly reduced prices. It was a great win for everybody.

We are stewards of a vision that can transform the world. When God calls, He always equips us to do the work that He calls us to do, even if we don't see how He is going to do it. Several years ago, one of our leaders in Reno, Nevada, Mike Reynolds, felt compelled to fight the ravages of methamphetamine. It was destroying his community and was responsible for much of the crime. He developed a TV documentary called *Crystal Darkness*, and then convinced leaders from all areas of civic life in Reno to join him and get this program aired at prime time with all other programming blacked out. It was a tall mountain to climb, but they did it and had a higher viewership than the Super Bowl! The calls overwhelmed the telephone banks that had been set up, but the community came together to face this evil.

Based on the success in Reno, several other FCCI members took up the call to repeat this in their city and state. They were successful in having *Crystal Darkness* programs in Las Vegas, Portland, Albuquerque, El Paso, Juarez, San Diego, Oklahoma City, and Seattle, all with the same impact. It was a stunning coming together of people who just wanted to help from all walks of life. It showed the power of service and the power to transform the world. If companies were run for Christ in every community, they could transform the world!

Money's Role

The bottom line of a company run for Christ is advancing the kingdom of God in and through the company in such a way as to spill over into the community and ultimately transform the world. The biblical picture of a company for Christ is found in Colossians 3:22–4:1. This is a picture of employees working diligently and performing their work as if they were working for Jesus, with sincerity of heart and full commitment. The employer is held to an equally high standard with the admonition to provide for his employees what is right and fair. There is an implied environment of love, trust, helpfulness, mentoring, honesty, and unselfishness. It's the image of a company that believes in the inherent worth of its people and creates kingdom value.

However, money is still necessary and important. There is no problem with money and profit as such, but there is a problem with the love of money, which is the root of all evil (1 Tim. 6:10). Money and finance have a vital role in the stewardship of any company, but as we've already seen, stewardship is much more than just money. Money must be managed effectively, and the way we handle money is a significant part of our witness. It's a complex and difficult walk with many gray areas, but fortunately, we have God's operating manual on how to navigate this rocky terrain. He gives us precise instruction on what to do. We're to pay fair wages, use just measures, and pay our bills on time (1 Tim. 5:18; Prov. 11:1). The Bible guides us on borrowing and lending decisions, partnerships, tithing, and many other areas of finance. We'll explore many of them in the next chapter.

GIVING

The steward must focus a significant part of his time on money, because it significantly impacts almost every area of running a business. Giving to religious organizations is the one area of managing finances that is unique to a Christian company. We are taught in our churches to follow Abraham's example and tithe our income. But as we study the New Testament scriptures, we find that Christian giving is voluntary. We don't have to do it, but it is a test of our sincerity and love. Larry Burkett used to say, "Giving is an outward indicator of an inward condition." So, what do you do? Should we worry about giving 8 percent or 10 percent or 15 percent? The answer is insignificant when we remember that God owns it all and we are just stewards or managers of what He has entrusted to us. We are responsible to manage it for His glory, not ours! It's all His, every dime of it. We must be so in tune with Him that we do exactly what He would have us do. It sounds a lot like, "What would Jesus do?" doesn't it?

We are CEOs and business owners and stewards, and we are charged with managing the assets of the King. We have to prayerfully decide many things about giving—where, how much, to whom, and how (benevolent fund, multiplied results, non-cash gifts, and so on). It's difficult. We do need to take care of our families, and we do need to send our kids to college. But there are lots of gray areas. It sounds a little ridiculous for us to keep 90 percent and give Him 10 percent, doesn't it? How do we decide? The answer is only by God's grace. We need prayer, counsel, and teaching on the difference between saving and hoarding, and ultimately God's confirmation that we're following His will.

God has blessed me with many godly counselors, as I've walked through the market these past forty-plus years. Terry Parker is one of those men. He founded an organization named National Christian Foundation to help people like you and me give more effectively and maximize our giving today and tomorrow and for the rest of our lives. They want to help us creatively and strategically "invest" more of God's money in building His kingdom. They are a wonderful resource to help God's people, and they have partnered with FCCI for many years to help our people. May God continue to bless our godly partners!

KEY CONCEPTS

- "The world is yet to see what God can do with and for and through and in a man who is fully and wholly consecrated to Him." – Henry Varley

- Stewardship is not just about managing money but everything God has entrusted to you.

- If you're a Christian CEO, then you're also a shepherd and are responsible for His sheep.

- Small company leaders need a council of advisors because there is wisdom in many counselors.

- You can't out-give God, so be generous!

STANLEY TAM
God Owns My Business

As a young man raised during the [Great] Depression era, Stanley Tam was hungry to succeed in the business world when he graduated from high school in 1933 in Lima, Ohio. He started out selling door-to-door, when he had an unexpected conversation with a potential customer. "One day I knocked at a door and a farmer's wife invited me in. For two hours, she talked to me about Jesus." Stanley was immediately captivated by the kind of "spiritual reality" she lived in, and six weeks later he came forward at church to be baptized. His life was now in God's hands. He worried less and began to trust God for the simple things in his life.

However, Tam was still an ambitious twenty-one-year-old, and he wanted to be a successful businessman. He'd become familiar with photographic plate technology and started a venture in reclaiming the silver that washed off the plates in the development process. Before long he realized that the distribution was more costly than the production, and he decided to call it quits. He headed home to his family farm, dejected and depressed.

But God stopped him during his travels and spoke to him. "It doesn't need to be a disappointment, Stanley. You don't need to go broke." In prayer, Stanley decided to keep the business going, and God would be his majority partner. He set up a trust where 51 percent of the profits went directly to and were used in the service of the gospel. He promised, "God, if you'll make this business succeed, I'll honor you in every way I possibly can."

A few years later, the business was going well and Stanley was in a meeting in South America. God spoke to him again. This time He said, "I want all of the business." Stanley struggled, but he decided it was better to obey God. When he got back to America, he asked his attorney to transfer all the ownership of the company over to the trust.

Stanley says there was never really a time when he doubted. He considers his business to be a pulpit to preach the gospel to his customers. And he suggests that they make their businesses pulpits for the gospel too. "Get all the businessmen that you know and go through your town and talk about how God owns your business. We have a lot of people who have given, say, 10 percent, 20 percent, or 30 percent to the Lord. You know, it's a joy. The only money you'll ever keep is what you give to God. When you get to heaven, there it is!"

When FCCI was in its early days, Bobby Mitchell heard about a man in Lima, Ohio, who had a big sign on his building that said, Christ is the Answer, who had written a book called *God Owns My Business*, and actually made a movie about the book. Needless to say, that grabbed his attention. He would send you the movie at no charge if you would agree to show it to twenty people. Bobby quickly sent off for the movie and was totally captivated by his story. He showed it many times before he had to send it back, but it left a lasting impact on him and the FCCI leaders. He then got the book and devoured it. Subsequently, he got many more copies of the book and passed them out to interested business owners."

Bobby went to visit Stanley, and Stanley began to share his story. "It was a story that is unlike any story I had ever heard,"

Mitchell says. "It was the story of his life. We started by talking about the sign and his passion for soul winning. The sign was a great witness and many had come to know the Lord by just riding down the road. He also put tracts that included a clear gospel message in every shipment. And then he pulled out a little book and said it was his goal to lead five people a day to the Lord. In stunned disbelief, I asked how he was doing on his goal. He opened his little book and after a moment, he said it had been a good year so far and that the previous month (April 1980), he had led 228 people to the Lord and was ahead of his goal for the year! Filing cabinets there in his office, filled to overflowing, evidenced the effectiveness of his soul-winning efforts."

At that time, Tam's companies were doing about $13 million per year, and the foundation was able to give $2 million per year to the mission field, plus they had planted over one hundred churches. As FCCI was beginning, Larry Burkett and Bobby Mitchell estimated that there were three hundred thousand Christian CEOs in America. We believed that if we could get thirty thousand to join FCCI, and if Stanley Tam's company represented the median size company in our estimates, we could change the world for Christ and complete the Great Commission in three years!

FCCI

CHAPTER 3

THE ULTIMATE AUTHORITY ON LIFE AND BUSINESS

Don't for a minute let [the Bible] be out of mind.
Ponder and meditate on it day and night,
making sure you practice everything written in it.
Then you'll get where you're going; then you'll succeed.

JOSHUA 1:8 MSG

Applied Ceramics has been developing and licensing technology to major companies around the world for the past thirty-five years. To do this we have established a process flow chart, designed factories, installed and operated equipment, trained staff, and commissioned or demonstrated technology. One project takes about eighteen months from start to finish. It is complex and elaborate. Therefore, every licensee absolutely requires one thing when we deliver the new technology—the user's manual. This manual sets forth in minute detail every aspect of the technology. No client would ever consider purchasing our product without it. Without the guidebook, they would not be able to operate the product after we've finished our installation and returned to our home offices.

Likewise, the Bible is the instruction manual we use when operating our businesses as a platform for ministry. It is God's inspired and inerrant word, the final authority, and the only absolute we have in life. Second Timothy 3:16 says, "All Scripture is God-breathed and is useful for teaching, rebuking, correcting and training in righteousness" (NIV). This applies to all areas of life—both personal and professional. It is the perfect manual, which reflects thousands of years of experience and unquestioned historical accuracy. The Founding Fathers demonstrated their strong faith in God and the Bible by clearly establishing our nation as a Christian nation. History shows that our Congress opened and closed those early sessions with prayer and Scripture reading, and even had all day prayer vigils in times of particular desperation. Many of our key leaders were committed Christians, and forty-four of the fifty-six signers of the Declaration of Independence were ordained ministers! The Bible was the primary text used by the people, the government, and the schools. It is America's godly heritage. Harvard, Princeton, and Yale continued in that tradition and extended the Bible into the marketplace, where it became the guide for doing business in America.

ESTABLISH A PURPOSE STATEMENT

At FCCI, we wrestled with the many different principles and concepts in the Bible, so we set out to establish a purpose statement. We went through a number of iterations over several years before we finally established that our purpose was:

> To equip and encourage Christian business own-
> ers and chief executive officers to operate their

businesses and conduct their personal lives in accordance with biblical principles in pursuit of Christ's eternal objectives.

For those of us who were there, we believe that this statement was God breathed and captured the essence of our call. It was not audible but close. We were all convinced that God had given it to us. We modified it slightly a number of years later, when we expanded to the current mission and vision statements, but we held firmly to the core concepts of that original statement. The phrase, "in accordance with biblical principles" meant that we were going to search God's Word for all the answers to our business and individual questions, and that we were confident we would find them there.

Our concept of biblical authority was further expanded when Francis Schaffer, a well- known theologian, philosopher, and evangelical thinker of the 1970s, wrote a book and film series entitled *How Should We Then Live?* The title was taken from the watchman passage of Ezekiel 33:10. The book captures the idea that the Bible is the only absolute that we have in life; everything else is relative. This is particularly important when dealing with high-powered leaders who readily give their own opinions and not necessarily God's. We can live by God's truth and be blessed, or we can reject it and suffer the consequences. Therefore, the foundation of biblical authority became and still is that the Bible is the ultimate guide for life and business and the only source of absolute truth.

STUDY THE BIBLE TOGETHER

After we established our purpose statement, our small group

of founders moved forward, confident that the Bible was the operating manual for our businesses. We met to study common business issues—hiring, firing, compensation, benefits, profit sharing, etc.—to see what the Bible had to say about them. One person was assigned to lead each week, and he would comb through Scripture to see what God had to say about that issue. Our discussions were lively, and we were learning and bonding together with a unified purpose.

Because we each came from different backgrounds and ran very different types of companies, we had the opportunity to see these principles applied in a variety of settings. Our companies became laboratories where we tested concepts, and the Bible was the guidebook that directed us. It became apparent that there were no magic lists, cookie-cutter formats, or one-size-fits-all scenarios that would make us "Christian companies." Each of us had to work these issues out with the Lord with fear and trembling (Phil. 2:12). The Bible was the foundation, but the fellowship, discussions, counsel, accountability, and testimonies from like-minded Christians were one way God chose to reveal His truth in Scripture to us. "As iron sharpeneth iron; so a man sharpeneth the countenance of his friend (Prov. 27:17 ASV)." It is truly a walk of faith.

Our little group of non-descript, small-business executives was far from perfect, and far from being well equipped for the task, but on February 26, 1980, we launched the Fellowship of Companies for Christ. Ninety-seven people attended our first conference at the Marriott in downtown Atlanta. It was a brand-new idea, and everyone was excited. These were people who wanted to make their companies their ministries. They wanted to join and be a part of what someone described as "a move of God." We weren't quite ready for that. We had no staff or resources other than what a few of us had chipped in. But God was ready, and FCC was birthed!

This first conference brought us instant exposure and many people who wanted to help. Bruce Wilkinson was one of those, and it was not long before he joined our Board. It immediately brought a new dimension to our group. The Board was still primarily composed of small-time business guys, but now it also had two ministry leaders: Bruce with Walk Thru the Bible, and Larry with Christian Financial Concepts. They were Bible scholars who came from very different perspectives. God had clearly answered our prayers beyond our wildest expectations and given us exactly what we needed. For the next several years, Bruce and Larry helped us refine the concepts we were developing with solid biblical undergirding. They also provided most of the teaching at our conferences, the tapes of which were subsequently turned into more training material for our members. Larry was focused on practical, nitty-gritty applications centered on finance and business, while Bruce focused on deep spiritual truths that formed the foundation for everything we did. It was all built on the solid foundation of God's Word. FCC owes a great debt of gratitude to Bruce and Larry for the spiritual leadership they provided in the early years of FCC.

In February 1983, Larry delivered a life-changing teaching to our meeting at Reach Out Ranch in Chattanooga. He spoke eight times and shared on the purpose and function of a Christian business, the basic minimums of a Christian business, how to identify godly success in a Christian business, biblical business planning; and how to make business decisions biblically. It was stunning! In one conference, with marathon sessions, he gave us a relatively complete picture of how to operate a company biblically! This series of talks responded to questions on practical issues businessmen like us faced every day. He addressed actual issues that had come up in counseling sessions with businessmen. He also focused on many of the business topics that the founders had struggled with in the early days prior to FCC. The answers came from God's operating manual. These talks were incredibly well received. So much so, in fact, that we began to use the tapes of these talks in our new member packets that went to every new member of FCC. They were foundational, and we believed that every member of FCC ought to have a set. Larry later turned this material into a best selling book entitled *Business by the Book*.

It's a radical thought to operate a business as a platform for ministry and honor to the Lord. It requires radical principles of business management that go beyond the basics of the Ten Commandments. *Business by the Book* is a guide for applying biblical principles in your company and in the workplace. It is God's answers to business questions. It focuses on basic biblical minimums in contrast to biblical business goals and extols the benefits of counsel in all things. It deals with critical policy decisions that face every manager, such as hiring, firing or compensation. It closes by addressing long-term structural and policy issues, transition, and retirement. It's a great book that has taught thousands of business people how to transform their businesses and marketplaces.

HAVE ADVISORS FOR
COUNSEL IN THE GRAY AREAS

Many issues business managers face are gray areas. It's difficult to open the word and immediately find a clear, black-and-white answer. Often a Christian business owner or CEO has to rely on general principles, like those found in the golden rule (Luke 6:31) or the parable of the Good Samaritan (Luke 10:30-37) to navigate the grays. The best way to handle these confusing problems is to ask, "What would Jesus do?" and then act accordingly. Clearly none of us really know, but the better we know God's Word, the better we can answer that question. And if we surround ourselves with men or women who are also spending quantity and quality time in Scripture, we can trust their counsel. Often times, these advisors have a much better perspective on our problems because they're not emotionally connected the way we are. So having this kind of support group can be a huge help.

EDUCATE YOUR EMPLOYEES
IN THE BIBLE

Over its nearly forty years, FCCI has touched more than 15,000 companies in one way or another. Many of them have found unique applications of the Bible in their business. One of the essentials of our fellowship is the sharing of our experiences with each other. This is the story of one man who turned to the Bible when he was in the middle of a crisis of belief. God blessed him and equipped him to help many others along the way. Isaiah 55:11 says, "My word shall not return unto me void, but it shall accomplish that which I please, and it shall *prosper* in the thing whereto I sent it" (KJV, emphasis added).

FCCI member Tom Hill is the president and CEO of Kimray, Inc., in Oklahoma City. Kimray manufactures and distributes valves and controls for the oil and gas industry. Tom was working as a senior manager in a family business, and there had recently been a lot of turnover in senior management. Unfortunately, not all of the new employees were good hires. One day Tom got a call from an irate woman. She was the wife of a man who worked the third shift at Kimray, and he often came home high on drugs. It was a wake up call for Tom. He had not known about this problem, but it caused him to carefully look at his whole operation. He was shocked to see that the shift in employees and the lack of character in many of the new hires was causing the company to spiral downward. Productivity and morale were down; profits were very slim; workers' compensation rates were at an all time high; and things were getting worse day by day. He didn't know what to do.

After studying the situation, he came to the conclusion that there was a common root cause—a lack of good character. The old adage "A bad apple spoils the barrel" was proving to be true. The question was how to change the bad apples to good apples. That could happen if his staff were taught God's Word and learned to apply it to their lives. But who would teach them? Was it his assignment? This was a call of God to use His Word for His glory. God will never call us or give us an assignment without equipping us.

There are no coincidences in the life of a Christian, and it was clearly no coincidence that at that time Tom was serving on the board of the Institute of Basic Youth Conflicts, Inc. It was also no coincidence that Bill Gothard, the president of that organization, had done a wonderful work developing material focused on character qualities found in the Bible. He had identified forty-nine biblical character qualities, and he allowed Tom to use this material to teach his employees.

God's Word did not return void. The people prospered *and* the company prospered. Tom taught one character quality a month, and the people responded. Morale went up; profits went up; and workman's compensation premiums went down. But that's not the end of the story. The transformation was so significant that Tom refined the process and launched the Character First ministry, which has a global reach and has helped thousands of businesses.

A company being run for Christ is not necessarily better than a secular company, but it is certainly different. Both need profit and growth, but in a God-honoring company, there needs to be a focus on kingdom fruit. We know from John 15:8 that God is glorified by the bearing of *much fruit*. This section of Scripture indicates that all Christians fall into one of four categories of fruit bearing—no fruit, fruit, more fruit, and much fruit. Therefore if we want to glorify God, we must bear much fruit. Not a little, but much! But first we need to understand what fruit is. Biblically, fruit is referred to in the contexts of conversion (salvation, Romans 1:13), character (fruit of the Spirit, Galatians 5:22, 23) and conduct (fruit of righteousness, Romans 6:21, 22). Apart from Christ we can do nothing, so to bear much fruit, we must walk in faith, which pleases God (Hebrews 11:6).

Navigating the Bumpy Road

Like Tom Hill, many members of FCCI regularly teach the Bible to their employees, who attend on a voluntary basis. In our company, we made a decision nearly forty years ago to hold a weekly Bible study on company time with refreshments for the purpose of leading people to Christ (salvation), helping all Christians new and old in our company to grow and mature in the Lord (sanctification), and to build a vision of how to help our community (service). We wanted to build God's absolute truth into our people. We've seen wonderful fruit in all three areas, but we've also experienced significant difficulties.

A number of years ago, we had a very bright young man named Robert Shaw who attended the study. Robert probed and challenged the Word and entered into intense discussions. There was no problem with that behavior. He did his job well, and we hoped that his participation in the Bible study would lead to his acceptance of Christ.

One day a man came to my office and asked to see me. He was from OSHA and had a major complaint (nineteen separate charges) against our company. I was staggered, but what he said next really shocked me. He said whenever he gets a complaint like this, he knows it's from a disgruntled employee. He recommended that I deny him entrance that day and fix as many of the items on the complaint as possible. He went on to say we couldn't keep him out of our factory forever, because the person who had filed the complaint was currently an employee. He would have to get a warrant and return in the morning with his team to inspect our facility. We prayed diligently and took his advice, working to fix as many things on the list as we could in the time available. The next morning the OSHA team arrived first thing as promised and started their inspection. It took some time, but we received a finding of no significant problems. He only fined us $150 for airborne nuisance dust. We rejoiced!

Over the next few weeks, we went on about our business with no significant issues. Then, out of nowhere, OSHA was back at our door with a new complaint. This time it was for religious discrimination. That week I had been teaching out of Colossians 3:23–4:1, which is about slaves and masters. I had substituted "employees" and "employers" in my teaching. The complaint said I was harassing our people and calling them slaves.

The OSHA agent said that the same employee had filed both claims, and they recommended that I pay him a $1,000 settlement to terminate his employment under a negotiated agreement. I readily agreed, and they brought in Robert Shaw. I had spent many hours pouring God's Word into Robert, hoping and praying that he might accept Christ. He was a bright young employee with a bright future. It was a real blow. But we put that behind us and moved on, expecting to never see Robert again.

Some ten years later, Robert came to the front office and asked to see me. I told the receptionist that I didn't want to meet with him. She returned, saying that he begged me to see him. I reluctantly agreed. Robert came in my office, sat down, and told me "the rest of the story." After he left our company, his life collapsed into drugs and drink, and he went down into the utter pit. There he remembered what I had taught him about Jesus Christ, and he accepted the Lord and was able to turn his life around. He came back to apologize for the horrible wrong he had done me and to thank me for leading him to Christ. He told me that he was now a business owner and had modeled his company after ours. To God be the glory! Applying the SSS Plan (Salvation, Sanctification, and Service) in our company bore much fruit. In this case, teaching God's Word as the guidebook of life and business caused the angels to sing.

God's Word is the ultimate authority. It can be applied in different ways by different people, but it never returns void. A parallel truth is that "in all things God works for the good of those who love him, who have been called according to his purpose" (Romans 8:28 NIV). But timing is key. Situations that look bad or even disastrous can turn out to be great blessings in God's perfect timing.

KEY CONCEPTS

- The Bible is the ultimate guide manual for life. Use it daily.

- God will never call us or give us an assignment without equipping us for the task to which He's called us.

- Trust God in the midst of your greatest problems, and He will deliver you in His time.

- There are no coincidences in the life of a Christian. Thank God and give Him the credit.

- God's Word never returns void, so rely on it!

DAVID RAE
A Long-Term View

David Rae's journey of running a "Christian business" started in the '80s. At that time, he was living in Canada and working as a vice president of Apple Computers Canada. David was a Christian and felt a call to be sharing his faith with others. God had blessed him with a boss who was a religious man—not necessarily a believer in the gospel of Christ, but accepting of David's faith and his willingness to share it with his coworkers.

But a good turn for David's career became a challenging stepping stone in his path toward workplace ministry—he was promoted to become the president of the company. All of a sudden, the brakes started to come on. There were a series of pressures that made sharing his faith at work difficult. To help him make his way through this difficult balancing act, he asked a friend who worked with the Navigators, a Christian ministry out of Colorado Springs, to walk alongside him, to be there for counsel and support, and to give advice. FCCI had already started strong in the United States, and this mentor introduced David to the concepts that FCCI was teaching about handling your money in a gospel-centric way and running your business on Christian principles. He started to apply these to his business practices at Apple Canada. Years later, he said, "It's kind of interesting to find myself working side by side with Larry Burkett and then eventually speaking at FCCI conferences. Our journeys were similar. A bunch of guys in Atlanta were wrestling with things that I was wrestling with in Canada, and there was this common person—being Larry—who had studied the Scriptures and had helped us both figure out this Christian business problem we were experiencing. God's got a funny sense of humor, for sure, in that whole thing."

Some of the pressures David faced were centered on the open, voluntary company Bible study that he led. When he was a vice president, it was going great. But once he became the company president, he sensed that his employees felt pressured to attend—that if they didn't show up, they might lose their jobs. He realized that his Christian influence wouldn't be best utilized in this heavy-handed way, so he backed off.

David decided his best Christian service to his company would be through prayer. He spent hours on his knees, praying for his business, his employees, their families, and the community they worked in. He was a support to those staff members under him who were also believers, allowing them to let their light shine for Christ in their roles at Apple.

One of the most significant truths David learned in those years was the idea found in Psalm 24:1, that "the earth is the Lord's, and everything in it" (NIV). Even though David was the president of one of the divisions of Apple Computers, he was just a steward for God. So he tried to figure out how he could be an effective steward in this public company. One way for him was to look at the core values. Establishing core values for his company is something he's continued to do over the years, and some of those values are:

- Psalm 24:01—The company belongs to God, and we are His stewards of it.

- 1 Corinthians 10:31—Abide by the highest moral and ethical standards possible.

- John 2:1–11—Celebrate continuous improvement in quality. Jesus turned water into "the best wine," and we should do the same with our products or services we create.

- Deuteronomy 24:15—Have honest and fair financial policies. If you pay your bills quickly, rather than a 30- or 60-day policy, your vendors will be happy to work with you in the future.

- Ruth 2—Give back to your community. At David's current business, Cables and Kits, they tithe 10 percent of their profit back into charitable organizations.

You'll see that these core values can have a direct biblical connection, but they can also be general moral concepts that all employees can embrace. Lead that way with passion and honesty. As David says, "The excellence of your work, based on your core values, will speak volumes about your faith because your faith is integrated with your work."

David encourages business owners to take the long view in work. The Bible is the foundation for that long view. People today want immediate results, but biblical success often takes many years. Proverbs 21:5 tells us, "The plans of the diligent lead to profit as surely as haste leads to poverty." FCCI is a fabulous place of learning, growth, camaraderie, and iron sharpening iron. It's smart to be accountable and to walk with people who have a focus on Christ and want to serve him by leading well in their businesses. You can do that through the network of believers at FCCI.

FCCI

CHAPTER 4

THE LIFEBLOOD
OF RELATIONSHIPS

And let us consider how we may spur one another
on toward love and good deeds, not giving up
meeting together, as some are in the habit of doing,
but encouraging one another—and all the more
as you see the Day approaching.

HEBREWS 10:24-25 NIV

Fellowship (between man and man or man and God) is the lifeblood of relationships. It is the deep bonding together of companions, groups, and companies. It may even go further to unite members of teams and states and countries. It requires unity and alignment and common goals or shared values. Certainly there is the fellowship or camaraderie when we unite to cheer on our team, whether it's Notre Dame or Alabama or Georgia Tech or the USA in the Olympics. It can even be euphoric for a moment, especially if we win, but when the game is over, regardless of whether we won or lost, the fervor wanes. This level of fellowship lacks consistent depth over a long period of time.

Godly fellowship has that depth and abundance and

richness of friendships that lasts a lifetime and is impossible to have apart from the Lord's involvement. This kind of deep relationship takes time to grow and develop. Take, for example, the disciples' relationship with Jesus. They worked and served closely with Christ for three years, but when they entered the upper room for the last supper (John 13:13), they were considered his *servants* and He was their Master. As the evening progressed and He shared deep eternal truths with them, He said they were no longer servants, but His *friends* (John 15:15). And finally, from the tomb, He sent word to them as *brethren* (John 20:17). From servants to friends to brothers, bonded for eternity. That is fellowship.

It's impossible to have this deepness of relationship apart from the Lord's involvement. Christian character is produced by the Holy Spirit, not by self-effort. It cannot be counterfeited. In *Life Together*, Dietrich Bonhoeffer wrote,

Christian brotherhood is not an ideal, which we must realize; it is rather a reality created by God in Christ in which we may participate. The more clearly we learn to recognize that the ground and strength and promise of all our fellowship is in Jesus Christ alone, the more serenely shall we think of our fellowship and pray and hope for it.[5]

In the 1970s, when the founders of FCC came together for the first time and made the choice to go God's way instead of man's way, none of us expected to come away from this group with life-changing friendships. We simply wanted to serve God in our businesses. But this living together, stumbling and searching and struggling together, has developed relationships that are fulfilling

5. Dietrich Bonhoeffer, *Life Together* (New York: Harper & Row, 1954) 30.

in a way that is rare. God called us to make our lives count, and He blessed our obedience to follow Him in fellowship with one another. The naming of the Fellowship of Companies for Christ International was not casual. Much prayer and discussion went into it. We had used the name Christian Business Fellowship in the meetings prior to launching FCC and had planned to continue using that name, however, Bob Dollar of Days Inn of America and several others took great exception to using the term "Christian Business," because a business cannot accept Christ and be saved. It was a simple truth, and we all agreed, but we were left without a name that described who we were. Much discussion and prayer ensued. We wanted our name to express that we were a group of companies that wanted to honor the Lord through our business. *Fellowship* seemed to be a perfect description, and we were all comfortable that our companies were for Christ. We had unity in that name, so we became the Fellowship of Companies *for Christ*—FCC for short. It seems like a very logical name now, but we struggled to get there. It has been a wonderfully descriptive name for us as we've grown into the largest peer-to-peer business ministry in the world.

We always had a heart for the world, but starting out we had no staff, materials, or resources, and our vision was limited. We barely understood that we were starting a ministry. We were just small business owners, coming together to learn how to operate these companies on biblical principles and to honor God through business. Initially we were centered geographically in the southeast, but word spread and we started to expand the ministry and the leadership. Smith Lanier and Jim Pursell ran larger companies and gave us great perspective when we added them to our Board. The ministry grew step by step as we added much needed staff, developed materials, and created resources. More people joined as we journeyed onward, and God continued to bless us and it was sweet. It took years for God to build our global vision into an official ministry, and it wasn't until the late 1990s that we added the "I" for *International* and became FCCI. Gradually it took root and became reality. Today, by God's grace, we touch more than sixty countries.

The name FCCI captured the essence of who we are. Many of us believe that God breathed the name into existence, just like FCCI's purpose statement. Today, we are a global fellowship, regardless of whether we say it in English, German, Spanish, or Chinese, and the fellowship is good. FCCI has evolved into a diverse group of companies in size and age and profession and geography. The one constant was and is that FCCI is built on God's principles, and if we apply them, they never return void, regardless of the culture or language. God's work done God's way always bears fruit. If we had truly understood that in the early days, we would have expanded internationally at an earlier time.

Oftentimes, CEOs and business owners are faced with decisions and problematic situations that are inappropriate for them to share with their employees, even their senior management. Even though they may have many friends, even close friends, inside their company, they frequently find that they don't have anywhere to turn when faced with a difficult decision. It is lonely at the top. But when business leaders have an outlet for Christian fellowship outside of their company, as they do within FCCI, they have a support system of peers they can lean on for solid, biblical feedback. It is invaluable to have safe and secure counsel from a Christian worldview.

Additionally, these groups provide accountability. Inevitably

I find that I receive a phone call from one of my group members in the days following a particularly difficult call I've had to make. They are encouraging me to stay firm in the faith, to be true to my biblical convictions, to remain in prayer, and to be an encouragement and light to my staff. This type of counsel is not available to most small businessmen. It is essentially a spiritual Board of Directors, on call 24/7. But this only comes when our members have committed to fellowship with one another.

WRESTLING IN THE WORD

When a new group of FCCI members is starting up, the best way for them to quickly discover a sense of connectedness and fellowship is by wrestling together in the Word. The FCCI ministry primarily works through wonderful conferences, small groups, excellent materials, so study of Scripture should be central to your meetings, as well as times of prayer and sharing. As you pour yourselves into the Bible, God will fill you with His Spirit of truth and unity. Eventually you, as a group, will come to the place where you are comfortable with Paul's command to "put away falsehood, let each one of you speak the truth with his neighbor, for we are members one of another" (Eph. 4:25 ESV). This speaking the truth into one another's lives is where fellowship starts.

PRINCIPLE OF UNITY

One of our earliest determinations at FCCI was that we would always operate on the principle of unity. No matter how far apart we started on an issue, we would be unified before we moved on. We haggled to our hearts content, but in the end we reached agreement. There was respect, freedom to disagree and seek the truth, and a deep love for each other. We were surprised to find that the relationships we were developing went beyond our small group as men and extended to our families, as our wives and children became friends as well. It was a very special time for us. When you're "doing life" with a group of brothers in close connection, this tends to spill over into all areas of your life. Once again, this principle of integrity—being one person in all areas of your life—comes to light. And the integrity of the individual was extended to the group, as we promised each other our commitment to group unity.

BE INTENTIONAL

Our original thought was to establish a conference ministry with a one-day conference in February, a two-day in May, and a three-day resort conference in September. Our goal was to share unique, biblical truth about how to run a company for Christ to a group of leaders who could then apply it. We wanted to give truth in the form of transferable concepts so that the members could use it in their companies, share it with others, and impact their communities. Initially we didn't plan to have organized groups or extensive materials, but by the end of 1980, it was clear that we had to move in that direction. The deepness of the fellowship and the need to stay connected between conferences drove that decision.

Two specific things happened that were pivotal in establishing the direction of the ministry. One was our decision to videotape every conference and the other was a startling *God moment* that happened at the first resort conference at

Point Clear, Alabama, in September 1980. God moved in unmistakable ways in both. It was an odd decision to video all the teaching sessions of every conference, especially since we had minimal structure, no resources, and no formal operating plan. But God would not let us reject the videotaping and, in fact, confirmed that we needed to move forward with it as a foundational operating principle for our conferences. It was an immediate blessing and provided the source of all our early teaching materials. Time and time again this has proven to be a great blessing and a great treasure that we are able to share with CEOs and business owners around the world. It was a way of extending fellowship to those who were not able to attend the conferences.

The second impact occurred at Point Clear and was equally unexpected, and probably more impacting. Forty-seven people attended that first resort conference. We were all very excited, but we didn't know what to expect. Bruce Wilkinson and Walt Wiley were our conference teachers. As we got into the sessions, Bruce explained that using a business as a platform for ministry was a new concept to him, and he had struggled with the subject matter. He shared that he had expected to go to the library, pull down some books on running a company for Christ, and develop his talks, but he was shocked to find that there were no materials on the bookshelves. None! So, he was struggling with what to deliver. Midway through the conference, he stopped in the middle of his message and said, "I've got it! I understand what you've been talking about, and I'm off target. We need God to show us how to operate a company for Christ." So we all got down on our knees and wept and cried as we went to the Lord in prayer. It was a stunning moment.

Those of us that were there that day were bonded forever, and we knew that something special had happened. FCCI was born of God that day and was tapped to bear much fruit globally. Bruce is a great Bible teacher and somehow got us through the conference using God's word to lay the foundation for some key concepts, but we all wanted more. We decided to have another conference in six weeks at another nearby resort, Callaway Gardens, to review what we had learned and try to determine where we were going. It's a tall order for a startup ministry with no staff or resources to put on a conference in a few weeks, but everyone was in favor of it, and God enabled us to do it. The bonding that had occurred over a few days was surprising, but we all knew that we had *unity* and were now a *fellowship*.

In a few short weeks, we reconvened at Callaway Gardens on October 28, 1980. Thirty of the original forty-seven came to a simplified day-and-a-half event, focused on continuing to lay the foundation of FCC. Everyone was excited to see what God had in store for us. It was a short, to the point meeting that had little entertainment or relaxation but was focused on the work at hand. Bruce had spent much time in prayer and many hours in the Word to flesh out the concepts that were emerging at Point Clear. There was much interaction during the messages, but foundational principles began to take shape. The teaching and interaction built our relationships. It was here for the first time that we heard that a company being operated to glorify the Lord is not necessarily better than a secular company, but it is *different*. It is different just as an apple is different from an orange; it has a different bottom line. As we've said before, all companies must make a profit, but a company being run for Christ must also bear spiritual fruit. Bruce went on to establish that the entire Bible can be broken down into three areas: Salvation, Sanctification, and Service, and that the results in these three areas comprise much of the spiritual profit of our companies. The Bible directs that we lead people to Christ; grow people up in the Lord; and serve our fellow man. These became the three S's of FCC and are still core to the ministry today. As we left Callaway, we knew that the ministry was established; that we had a fellowship; and that our companies needed to focus on bearing spiritual fruit.

Many of the relationships in FCCI occur within groups, as couples, one on one, or at the conferences. However some relationships are also built in more unique ways. Kent Humphreys was a warrior for the Lord and a great leader for FCCI. He was comfortable on the platform and could bring message after message with true excellence. He was a visionary who had almost unlimited energy and drive, but he also had compassion and empathy for others. He had a ministry of caring, and was a great example of an intentional friend. He wrote letters, visited the friendless, and most importantly he was a man of prayer. As a quiet warrior, he prayed for an extensive group of people who had shared their needs with him. I once wondered if he could ever pray for all the hundreds of requests he received. One day I got my answer.

My son was an adult, single, and lonely. He sent Kent a postcard, asking if he would pray for him to find a wife. We never heard anything specifically from Kent about this request, and life went on as usual. Several years later, my son had met a lovely woman and they married. Not long after the wedding, my son received a letter from Kent. Inside was the postcard with my son's prayer request. Across the face of the card, Kent had written, Prayer answered! His thoughtfulness was deeply meaningful, not only to my son and his new bride, but also to my wife and myself. Intentional friendship creates a deep bond, and it has a ripple effect that extends beyond the person you're caring for and blesses many others in its wake.

FELLOWSHIP THROUGH MISSIONS

Throughout the New Testament, we see the close-knit community of the believers in Jesus Christ. These deep relationships were formed through the missions trips of Paul and Timothy, and they were maintained by the fact that these individuals shared faith in Christ together. They communicated regularly, and they suffered together. Modern long-distance friendships are very similar. One of FCCI's long-time members, Cade Willis, felt God's call to move his family from Georgia in the southern USA to Singapore to reach ten unreached people groups in that part of the world. Not long after their move, Cade was overwhelmed at the hunger for Christ in the Singaporean marketplace. So, he set up a series of meetings and invited a few leaders to see if the message of FCCI would resonate in Asia. I was grateful for the chance to attend.

The trip was a non-stop experience, sixteen hours a day with only time for five-minute power naps on rare occasions. We spoke twenty times and met with forty-three key marketplace leaders. We had a wonderful dinner overlooking the Indian Ocean from the home of the Calamari King. We preached to several thousand in several different churches. The response was beyond anything we could have imagined.

The fields were truly ripe to harvest. By the end of our trip, our question had become, not whether the FCCI message resonated in Asia, but how were we going to respond to the clear call of God to work in Asia?

The unity we shared in our vision and the difficulty we shared in persevering through such an exhausting journey was the basis for friendships that have lasted through the years. Working together in missions is a great foundation for building relationships. "May the God who gives endurance and encouragement give you a spirit of unity among yourselves as you follow Christ Jesus, so that with one heart and mouth you may glorify the God and Father of our Lord Jesus Christ" (Rom. 15:5-6 NIV).

KEY CONCEPTS

- Jesus had intimate relationships with His disciples, but their relationship didn't move from that of servants to friends until the upper room, and they were called brothers after His ascension. True intimacy of fellowship takes time!

- It's lonely at the top. Make sure you're in an accountability group, and have a council of advisors. Who are you in fellowship with?

- You'll know my disciples by their love, one for another. Are you practicing the principle of unity?

- Great growth occurs when you are doers of the word and not hearers only. Go on an FCCI mission trip.

BERTHOLD G. STUMBERG
Making Your Life Count

My friend Bert Stumberg was a great guy. He was old enough to be my dad, but he was one of my best friends. He was likeable, jovial, and interested in virtually everything. He was relational, wise, and a great listener. He was also a great leader, and most importantly, a true friend. Bert was my business partner and co-founder of FCCI. He and his wife, Shirley, had wonderful relationships with many, and they were devoted grandparents to twenty-one grandchildren. But Bert was so much more than his resume. Hopefully in the telling of this story, you'll catch a glimpse of who Bert really was. He may be best described as *the prototypical FCCI man*.

Bert's Christian walk began in a most unusual way. As a soldier in World War II, Bert was captured by the German forces for a second time. He was handed a shovel and told to dig...*his grave*! As he dug, he looked down into the black hole and was sure of death. Suddenly, he and his fellow prisoners heard a noise, and Bert dropped down to his knees. He said a quick prayer and told the Lord that if He would just get him out of this, he would serve Him forever. When he looked up, his German captors were gone. Bert took off. His commitment to the Lord on that battlefield was real, and he had good intentions, but when he got back home "he left the Lord in Germany."

As a young man back from the war, Bert set out to make his fortune. He was a textile engineer with a degree from Georgia Tech and was very successful, owning his own business within a few years. He was a churchgoer and a giver, but he was not walking with the Lord. He looked pretty good in the world's eyes, but there were some chinks in his armor.

Fast forward a few years and Bert bought another company. It was a high-tech ceramic company that he thought he could turn around and give to his son to run. Unfortunately, after a few years, the company declined significantly, and he had to turn to some consulting help.

That's where our friendship began. *I was the consultant*. I evaluated the company and wrote him a report on how to fix it. He hired me to fix the problems and teach his son how to run it. I had only two conditions: I had to be able to run it as a Christian company, and I had to have a $100,000 line of credit available to me. The money was no problem, but he wanted to know what this "Christian company" concept was all about. I told him I was working on it and didn't really know, but I was going to tithe the profits, teach a Bible study, have a prayer room, and put a cross in the logo. He thought for a minute and said, "We're not making any money now, so if we start making money and I get to keep 90 percent, that's a lot better than nothing." We were off to the races! Little did I know the events of the next few weeks would shape us both for the rest our lives.

Bert's son, BG, was a few years younger than I was, and he had just given Christ Lordship in his life. Bert told me that his son "had gone off the deep end." He wanted to know if I could "help" him. I said I could, and I began to disciple BG and take him to a men's Bible study. Several weeks later, Bert thanked me for helping his son and asked me what I was doing? I said, "Let me show you," and I took him to the Bible study. He was fifty-three and a little out of place because this was a young guys' (ages 25-40) discipling Bible study. However on that particular day, it was hell, fire, and brimstone. The next thing I knew, Bert was weeping on the sofa, having just met the Lord that he left on the battlefield in Germany.

That started a lifelong friendship and co-laboring in the marketplace between Bert and myself. He was hungry and eager to learn, and he made up for lost time. He particularly wanted to know about running a Christian company and caught the vision instantly. We were totally in sync and joined at the hip for life.

As God brought the FCCI founders together, Bert exerted strong leadership. When we started FCC, we modeled it after a trade association that he had been a member of. We were a conference ministry, with a one-day in February, a two-day in May, and a three-day resort meeting in September. He became the first Chairman and led us for the next sixteen years. Shortly thereafter, he sold his business and joined the FCCI staff full time. His handprints are all over the ministry.

Bert was a lot of fun—he'd call our conferences together with a horn!—but he also had a more serious side and imparted a lot of wisdom to our ministry. For example, he insisted that we videotape the conferences, even though we couldn't really afford it. It became one of the wisest things we ever did because it provided us with the teaching material we would so desperately need. He had deep wisdom and foresight, and we owe him a tremendous debt of gratitude.

Bert was a great Chairman for FCCI, but there was so much more to him. He epitomized what an FCCI man is.

When he had his second conversion, he could not identify anyone in his family, except his son BG, or at his business who had a vital relationship with the Lord. So he set out to change that. He put a six-foot tall cross on the side of his business and proclaimed Christ to all who would hear. When he sold the business, he had sixty employees. All sixty of those employees knew the Lord; all of his immediate family knows the Lord; and each of his twenty-one grandchildren know the Lord, plus many others. He was a giver of what God had entrusted to him, and he was found faithful.

Shirley gave Bert a wonderful surprise eightieth birthday party with about one hundred family and friends in attendance. BG was the MC. Toasts were made, and fun was had by all. BG closed the party with one last poignant story. Not long after Bert's second conversion, BG passed by his Dad's home office and found his Dad weeping for all the years he had wasted. He ministered to his Dad from Joel 2:25, which says that God "will restore the years the locusts have eaten." BG closed the party as he looked out on the audience, pointed to us, and said, "You are the years God restored!" Bert was a man who had a great heart for the Savior, who made up for lost time, and who made his life count.

The Founders:
(left to right)
Bobby Mitchell,
Jim Moye,
Bill Leonard,
Larry Burkett,
Thomas Harris,
Ben Lively,
Bert Stumberg

The original sign up sheet of **the very first organizational meeting** of what became FCCI (held at Edwards Pie Company). Bill Leonard and King Grant attended the first meeting, but failed to sign this sheet.

Stanley Tam's advertisement *(right)* showing the six foot high cross on his building along with Christ is the Answer. It includes an offer to sell you his book, **God Owns My Business,** for $2.95 each in lots of ten, and send his movie of the same title free of charge if you agree to show it to 25 people on your premises and return it the next day.

An early Board meeting *(below),* at Bert and Shirley's house at Lake Martin. The attendees left to right and front to back were Darlene Wilkinson, Gwin Harris, Judy Burkett, Jerry Woodward *(first row),* Bruce Wilkinson, Thomas Harris, Larry Burkett, John Woodward, Judy Camp *(second row),* Shirley Stumberg, Sara Moye, Sue Mitchell, Sandy Leonard, Chris Pursell, Betty Lively *(third row),* Bert Stumberg, Jim Moye, Bobby Mitchell, Bill Leonard, Jimmy Pursell, Ben Lively, Stan Vermeer, George Brown *(fourth row).*

The original Executive Committee of FCCI *(below),* L-R: Bill Leonard, Jim Moye, Bert Stumberg, and Bobby Mitchell; plus our first employee (Charlotte Estep) and our first resort speaker (Bruce Wilkinson) at Point Clear, Alabama in 1980.

CC was founded out of a hunger to honor God through our businesses."

Bobby Mitchell presents Bert Stumberg with the "horn," *(left)* as Bert steps down as Chairman of the Board in 1995.

The original Affirmations of the Fellowship of Companies for Christ *(right)* prior to the I and International

The Affirmations of the Fellowship of Companies for Christ

Leadership

The chief executive officer believes...

I ...Jesus Christ is the son of God and has personally accepted His gift of salvation.

II ...the Bible is God's inspired revelation to man and endeavors to live in obedience to its principles and commands.

III ...the Chief Executive Officer is a member of good standing in a local church and supports the work of Christ through the church by his time, talents, and financial resources.

Corporate

This company strives...

I ...to share the Gospel of Jesus Christ with its employees and also its customers, competitors, suppliers, and any other business contacts.

II ...to take an active part in the development of the spiritual life and Christian testimony of its employees.

III ...to operate in accordance with the commands and principles of Scripture in dealing with its finances, in handling its personnel, and in administering its policies.

IV ...to give regularly a portion of its financial and personnel resources in meeting various Christian responsibilities in accordance with Scripture. This pertains to the needs of its employees as well as others, and may be accomplished through direct contributions or through contributions to agencies and ministries.

Doctrinal

This company believes...

I ...there is one God, eternally existing in three persons: the Father, the Son, and the Holy Spirit.

II ...the Bible is God's written and inspired revelation to man and is the primary authority for man's life.

III ...in the deity of Jesus Christ, His virgin birth, sinless life, miracles, death on the cross to provide for our redemption, resurrection, bodily ascension into heaven, present ministry of intercession for us, and His return to earth in power and glory.

IV ...in the personality and deity of the Holy Spirit, in His power to perform the miracle of the new birth in unbelievers and to indwell believers, enabling them to live a godly life.

V ...man was created in the image of God, and because of sin was alienated from God — that alienation can be removed only by accepting, through faith, God's gift of salvation which was made possible by Christ's death and resurrection.

VI ...Jesus Christ is the Head of the Church, and that all believers are to assemble together regularly for worship, for edification through the Scriptures, and for mutual encouragement.

VII ...Jesus Christ commanded all believers to proclaim the Gospel throughout the world and to disciple men of every nation. The fulfillment of the Great Commission requires that all worldly and personal ambitions be subordinated to a total commitment to "Him who loved us and gave Himself for us."

Top/right: The Bible tells the story of the potter and the clay in meaningful detail. As a ceramic company, Applied Ceramics developed this card and sent it along with a tape that presented the gospel through a description of the ceramic process. It was a Thanksgiving card that went to all of our employees, their families, customers, suppliers, competitors, and other business contacts. It was a significant outreach that touched thousands of people. The response was overwhelming. It's an example of one of the ways that we've consistently reached out to others.

Left, top: **Manuel Espina and the Mayor of Almolonga with his wife** and the super sized carrots of God's harvest blessing. *Left, bottom:* **The Missionary Journey to Guatemala** to investigate George Otis' report on the transformation of Almolonga. The U.S. team pictured above includes James Massa, Pat McGrath, Sue Mitchell, Bobby Mitchell, and Chuck Bentley.

This is the only time that we've ever had **four Presidents or former Presidents in one picture surrounded by other Board members and the wife of an outgoing President** *(above)*. The front row *(L-R)* includes Kent Humphreys, Janet Hunter, Doug Hunter, Bobby Mitchell, Terence Chatmon with Mike Amorosa; Pat McGrath, Jim Moye, Jim White, Jorg Knoblauch, and Marian Noronha on the second row. **The Board** *(below)* is the keeper of the vision and as such is responsible for the History, Structure, and Strategy of the ministry. As throughout all of our history, the board has great camaraderie, bonding and wisdom and provides vibrant leadership.

Present at this **FCCI dinner** are *(above, L-R)* Howard Dayton, Bobby Mitchell, Ron Blue, Bev Dayton, Terry Parker, Paula Parker, Bert Stumberg, Shirley Stumberg, Sue Mitchell, Judy Blue, Henry Blackaby, Marilynn Blackaby, Bill Leonard, Judy Burkett, Larry Burkett, and Sandy Leonard.

As we look at new tools, technologies, and personalities, it is important to look back to Jesus' first sermon and remember how important it is to build on a good foundation. **Sue and I** have traveled this road for forty years, and we can testify that a good foundation has been laid. As we hand the baton to the leaders of the future, we look forward expectantly to a time of mega fruit bearing.

CHAPTER 5

INTEGRITY

> Show yourself in all respects to be a model
> of good works, and in your teaching show
> integrity, dignity, and sound speech that cannot
> be condemned, so that an opponent may be put
> to shame, having nothing evil to say about us.
>
> TITUS 2:7-8 ESV

After I accepted Christ as a young businessman, I realized that I lacked integrity. My actions didn't necessarily match what I said I believed. As I looked around, I wondered if anybody really had integrity. I started to search diligently, but I couldn't find a man of true integrity, someone who walked his talk twenty-four/seven. Certainly there was no one who measured up to the extremely high bar that I had set. Then one day, I realized that my father was such a man. He was a good man, with a firm conviction to maintain his biblical moral code at all times. He did what he said he would do, and he did what was right. I could count on what he said. He was the same person in the morning as at night or on the weekend. He was the same regardless of who was present. He treated the janitor the same as the president of the bank. There was no arrogance or condescension with him. He was not perfect, but he was humble, consistent, and God-fearing in every circumstance.

Those are the characteristics of a man of integrity. They are very rare, but when you meet one, you'll know it right away. Because men of integrity seek no glory for themselves, their business success is generally understated. Jesus described such a man in His first sermon when He admonished us to, "Let your light so shine before others, so that they may see your good works and give glory to your Father who is in heaven" (Matt. 5:16 ESV). Put simply: *Godliness + Consistency + Humility = Biblical Integrity*. Likewise, for a company to successfully operate as a platform for ministry, it must have integrity.

If you've taken the time to read this book, then you're probably a person who wants to live with integrity and honor in your life. But where do we start? Integrity doesn't develop overnight, and it doesn't happen by accident. We have to be intentional about integrity, just as we have to be intentional about developing fellowship and organizing our companies to be Christ centered. Here are some steps that will put you on the path toward living a life of integrity.

WRITE A STATEMENT OF FAITH

On my very first day in college, my instructor told us to listen up, because he was going to teach us the most important thing we would learn during our college years: "You must first define the problem if you want to solve it!" Without question, this stepping back, refocusing, and evaluating the problem can be incredibly helpful.

It is helpful in solving any problem you face, in any area of your life. It is simple but remarkably effective. It is not just helpful in academics but on your job, in relationships, and even your walk with the Lord. However, it is essential that you expand that simple truth to know what you believe, if you want to walk that belief out in your life. The best tool to help you evaluate your beliefs is a statement of faith. It could be as simple as a theme verse from the Bible, a personal purpose statement, or one of the creeds from church history (check out the Apostles' Creed or the Nicene Creed as examples). In our company, every employee carries a card that states our vision and core values. At FCCI, we have a statement that describes the leadership, corporate, and doctrinal affirmations we ascribe to.[6]

It is important that you take the time to write a personal statement that guides your life and that you review often. It might be purely a statement of faith that describes your understanding of God, your moral values, and your expectations for Christian living; it should focus on what the Christian life should look like. On the other hand, it might be a statement that blends your spiritual heart with your work life. I believe that one of the great problems in America today is that most of us compartmentalize our faith and we also compartmentalize our work, and they don't meet. It is absolutely critical that they be integrated if we, or our companies, are to have integrity. This cannot be a statement that we write out and keep in the desk drawer. We must refer to this statement in both good times and bad. It is particularly helpful when

6. You can read our full statement of faith ("*the Affirmations*") in Appendix C of this book.

you're facing a confusing or difficult situation. Being clear on your beliefs will help you know how to move forward in a way that glorifies Christ.

As with the other foundational concepts of FCCI, these affirmations were God breathed. They were the product of much prayer, alongside debates and struggles. Some of these disagreements were comical in hindsight. The first point under the corporate affirmations says, "The chief executive officer strives through the company . . . to share the gospel of Jesus Christ with its employees and also its customers, competitors, suppliers, and any other business contacts." We could not come to agreement on this point, because one member of the board just could not get comfortable with praying for his competitors. We went round and round on this for quite a while. Finally, the dissenting board member relented and agreed, and we had unity. As we left the room, the previously dissenting member was heard to mutter, "I didn't say what I would pray for my competitors, only that I would pray for them." Clearly, we were a work in progress.

STAY ALERT

Integrity is all about doing the right thing when no one is looking or when your indiscretion would never be discovered. It's doing the right thing regardless of the results, even when it hurts. In his first epistle, Peter warns us, "Be self-controlled and alert. Your enemy, the devil, prowls around like a roaring lion looking for someone to devour. Resist him, standing firm in the faith, because you know that your brothers throughout the world are undergoing the same kind of sufferings" (1 Pet. 5:8–9 NIV).

All of us face challenges to our integrity virtually every day. Many times we don't recognize integrity issues as they are developing. They can be as simple as whether or not we'll be respectful to our subordinates, if we will lose our patience with a worker on our factory line, or if we realize we forgot to give our client a discount they deserved whether we will just let it slip. These things just catch us by surprise. Oftentimes there are little warnings that we miss.

Song of Solomon 2:15 says, "Take us the foxes, the little foxes that spoil the vines; for our vines have tender grapes." The king renowned for his wisdom is telling us to pay attention to the little issues in life and deal with them, because if we don't, they will cause bigger and bigger problems. Those "little foxes" can spoil the entire production for our year if we let them slide. And the little sins that creep into our habits can destroy our character if we don't recognize them for what they are. God wants to shine his light into our lives, so that the "little" issues become clear. Are you faithful in the little things?

EXERCISE YOUR INTEGRITY MUSCLES

Even when we face black-and-white issues and our course of action is clear, it can still be difficult. It takes strength of convictions and courage to be men and women of integrity. We must be committed and intentional in our integrity. It will not develop casually. You must exercise those muscles early and often, making the right choice in all situations— especially when the situation you face falls more in a gray area and the outcome wouldn't be devastating to your company.

Employees should follow company policy at all times, not only when there's a threat of being caught. If this is the habit of your company, then you'll be in the right position to make the difficult decisions when they need to be made.

COMMUNICATE CLEARLY

Many years ago, when our company was small and struggling, I had a key supervisory employee that I mentored while he went through personal bankruptcy; we worked through Larry Burkett's principles in the Christian Financial Concepts material (now Crown Financial Ministries). We had worked out a budget and our bank had agreed to make him a loan so that he could reestablish his credit, as long as we would continue to oversee the process. He had picked out two cars that he was interested in and he came to me for advice on which to buy. We discussed his needs and the price, looking at which one might be a better fit for him. Finally, after he had shared his thoughts, I made a recommendation as to which car he should buy. We concluded and he headed back to the plant. As he left he bumped into another employee and promptly told him that, "Mr. Mitchell was making him buy *the wrong car!*" It taught me a great lesson as a leader, to speak precisely and be careful about what I say. When I make any suggestions or recommendations about their personal lives, I need to be very clear that the decision is *theirs* to make. This was a little fox.

This man went on to work for the company nearly forty years, and he was a great friend and valued employee. But through my relationship with him I learned that communication is often difficult, so take care.

PERFORM REGULAR SELF-EVALUATIONS

So, as men and women seeking to operate companies for Christ, that brings us to a significant question. Is there a behavioral difference between a secular businessman and a Christian businessman? Can you tell the difference? Remember, behavior always reflects belief. Your actions and motives give a clear picture of what you believe. The bottom line of a company being run for Christ *must be different* than a secular company's bottom line. Eternal principles and the focus on salvation, sanctification, and service to build the kingdom of God must be apparent in a Christian businessperson. If it isn't apparent, then the company is immature or completely off track in its journey to honor God.

As company leaders, we need to continually search our hearts to see if they are pure. We can do this by asking meaningful questions. At FCCI we encourage all of our members to ask themselves these three questions to check the health of their company's commitment to Christ:

1. Do we act with integrity in every circumstance? Why or why not?

2. Do our actions and decisions reflect our statement of faith? How or how not?

3. Do our clients, customers, and competitors know that we are a Christ-centered company? Why or why not?

These are daunting questions, but when we scrutinize our commitment to Christ, we can see our weaknesses more clearly and know where we need to grow. We need to understand that even more difficult questions might come up as we go down this path.

CONFESS . . . IMMEDIATELY!

None of us are perfect. Every last one of us will fail in our roles as leaders at some point—"For all have sinned and fall short of the glory of God" (Rom. 3:23 NIV). We tend to classify sin as big or small, but God tells us that even the smallest sin will keep us out of heaven. It can be embarrassing, even humiliating, to fall into sin. When you're the leader of a company and you've made a sinful decision, it can quickly become public knowledge.

King David, one of the greatest leaders of early Israel, knew a little about this. After he'd committed adultery with the wife of one of the men in his military, the prophet Nathan came to him and made his sin clear in David's eyes. He sat down in repentance and wrote this psalm,

> Have mercy on me, O God,
> according to your unfailing love . . .
> Wash away all my iniquity
> and cleanse me from my sin.
> For I know my transgressions
> and my sin is always before me . . .
> Cleanse me with hyssop, and I will be clean;
> wash me, and I will be whiter than snow.
> (Ps. 51:1–2, 7 NIV)

We must be ever vigilant. In those moments when we have fallen, it is extremely important that we address integrity issues immediately. Do not let your sin fester. Deal with it! Go to your fellowship of other leaders and receive their counsel, confess your sins, and work to make the situation right again.

FORGIVE

As business leaders, we should take caution from the parable of the unforgiving servant, found in Matthew 18:21–35. This servant owed his king a great debt, which the king graciously forgave. But when the servant went back to his workplace, he found the first man who owed him money and demanded repayment. When the man couldn't repay, he had him thrown in jail. When the king discovered this ungrateful servant's response, he had him also thrown in jail, where he would be tortured until he could repay.

In this story, we are the servants who have been forgiven much. Let us beware of the danger of refusing to forgive—if a man of integrity fails to forgive, even when he has been unjustly or terribly wronged, he is no longer a man of integrity. And he could face grave consequences for his hardness of heart. "If you do not forgive others their trespasses, neither will your Father forgive your trespasses" (Matt. 6:15 ESV). Forgiveness is essential if we are to have God's power in our ministries or our lives. Remember what David tells us, "If I had cherished sin in my heart, the Lord would not have listened" (Ps. 66:18 NIV). The value of a clean heart goes hand in hand with the life of a man of integrity.

INTEGRITY IN ACTION

Living with integrity is challenging, and the issues we face can be so significant they just overwhelm us. They can multiply and seem bigger than life itself, yet even so, the irony is that we often do not see them coming at all. It sometimes takes a long time for these issues to run their course.

This happened with us once at Applied Ceramics. Our business is in the development and commercialization of technology through large, international partners. The first international venture we undertook was in 1982 with a midsize German company. We had an option to buy control of one of their U.S. subsidiaries in a joint venture agreement. The German company was technology rich, and the venture was a perfect fit for us. But we failed to see that we actually had a breeding ground for little foxes.

What we were not aware of is that, for reasons of personal gain, the manager of the subsidiary didn't want the venture to go through. After the initial excitement of startup, we had problem after problem. We tried to operate as a God-honoring company but had countless conflicts. We were losing significant amounts of money and having to lay people off. It seemed like everything we tried failed. When we didn't think it could get any worse, the EEOC showed up at our door and cited us with nine complaints of religious discrimination. We were accused of terminating people because they were not the right kind of Christian.

We hold Bible studies in all of our facilities, but we're extremely careful to obey U.S. laws—these studies are *totally* voluntary. In them, we teach cardinal Christian doctrine and avoid going down rabbit trails of secondary doctrine, as this varies so much between denominations. We want them to be accessible to *all* Christians.

As we looked more closely at the complaints, we found

that every one referenced our FCC doctrinal affirmations and tried to make the point that all Christians are not the same. It became obvious there was collusion in the claims. We met with every claimant and explained how careful we had been to operate within the law, and that the purpose of the study was to help build strong character in our people. Four claimants withdrew their claims.

So, off we went to a state of Tennessee courtroom to address the other five complaints. The plaintiffs presented no real evidence against us. When we presented our purpose and intent and care in keeping the law, the judge ruled very strongly in our favor and dismissed these cases. Unfortunately, even on a strong dismissal, the judge had to offer all of the plaintiffs a right-to-sue letter that would take the case to the Federal court. Four of the five decided that they had had enough and withdrew, but the last one, our general manager, decided to proceed. We had sent this particular manager to a training course to learn how to deal with the EEOC, and now he was using what he had learned against us.

He found a lawyer who was willing to take his case on a contingency basis in the hopes of a very profitable win. Again, no evidence was presented against us; the testimonies on our behalf were well received. The judge strongly reprimanded the plaintiff for wasting the court's time with a frivolous lawsuit and rendered a scathing opinion in our favor.

But the story does not end there. This manager convinced one of our key engineers in Atlanta to partner with him and go into competition against us. They took all of our sales records and our confidential technology documents. We immediately sued them to get our information back. It was an open and shut case, and they were looking at jail time in addition to making restitution. It was here that this story took a strange twist.

Two years earlier, our company had an overnight retreat at Callaway Gardens. Bruce Wilkinson was the Bible teacher and shared about developing a closer walk with Christ. Our manager from Chattanooga had gone on that retreat and had heard the teaching. When we were proceeding to take strong legal action against him, he approached Bruce and claimed to be a Christian and said that Christians cannot sue each other based on what Bruce had taught at the prior retreat. Bruce acknowledged that to be true and called me to discuss the matter.

I declared there wasn't a chance he was a Christian. I had just traveled all over Europe with him and shared the gospel with him as we traveled. As far as I could tell, he had no concept that Jesus had died for him and paid the price for him to have eternal life. Bruce then asked a stunning question. Is there a one in ten thousand chance that he is a Christian? I was quiet for a long period of time when I heard myself say, "Yes." The answer then came back immediately, "You can't sue him!" Wow, I had been significantly wronged and it hurt, but God asked me to lay it all aside. We went through the Christian Conciliation Service shortly thereafter.

We selected a three-panel board that was acceptable to both of us. We prayed, meditated, studied the Word, and discussed the merits of the case, guided by the board. And then we repeated the process, again and again, hour by hour until God softened our hearts. Finally, some eighteen to twenty hours later, it was finished. It was emotional and painful, and I wasn't sure what had happened, but I had let it go. I knew that I had submitted to the Lord, seeking to be a man of integrity. It was a higher objective than to win the game. It expanded my platform to be able to share various aspects of this story with others. Sometime later God also used our EEOC testimony in another legal skirmish to help defeat a provision the government was proposing to make it illegal to have a Bible on your desk at work. It preserved our freedoms, at least for another day. "And we know that in all things God works for the good of those who love him, who have been called according to his purpose" (Rom. 8:28 NIV).

KEY CONCEPTS

- Integrity comes from the word *integer*, which means "complete." Be one person in every circumstance, consistent and never changing.

- There is a cost associated with being a man of integrity.

- Trust God throughout the whole process, because it often takes a long time. His ways are always the best, even when they don't seem like it.

- Make sure that you are faithful in the little things. Remember that the little foxes spoil the vine.

RALPH AND WALT MELOON
Bold Leadership

Ralph Meloon, Sr., is a spry 94-year-old and former CEO and Chairman of the Board of Correct Craft, the first company to commercially manufacture ski boats. Ralph's dad started the company in 1925 as Florida Variety Boat Company and changed the name to Correct Craft in 1947. Ralph has been serving the company in a variety of different positions for more than forty years. He still goes to the office daily.

Ralph is known for his love for the Lord, and for treating all people equally, a respect for people that is only born out of God's love for His creation. Wendell Guthrie, who attends church in Orlando, Florida, with the Meloons testifies of their integrity. "When I was a child, my dad worked at Correct Craft. He broke his foot and he could not work for some time. My mom was very worried about how we were going to make it, because in those days there wasn't any insurance. But every Friday until my dad could return to work, a Meloon family member showed up at our house and gave my dad a check. They didn't have to do that, but that's just the kind of people they are."

The Meloons' love for Christ is not something you'll discover only after lengthy conversations or years of knowing them; it's something they boldly profess to any who will listen. Their Correct Craft factory proudly displays large banners of their beautiful boats, and the captions below read Building Boats to the Glory of God. Ralph shares, "We're not here to build boats.

We are here to lead people to Christ. We build boats to pay the expenses."

This passion for integrating faith and vocation isn't limited to a country with such freedom of religion as the United States enjoys. When he was contacted by China about purchasing boats and starting a waterski program, just four years after communist leader Mao Tse Tung left power, Ralph told the government official that he was willing to accept the invitation on one condition—that they provide a church for him to attend on Sundays. The government agreed. He passed out Christian evangelistic leaflets to people along the streets, and a Chinese doctor came to know Christ.

Over the years, Correct Craft has hosted a catered chapel on Tuesdays during lunch hour. Attendance is voluntary, but nearly fifty employees regularly attend. Employees testify that working there has been a life-changing experience that has benefitted not only the employees but also their families. Some of the chapels train employees in certain areas of their life, such as the *Raising Kids God's Way* study or the Dave Ramsey Financial Peace University. These meetings have even given way to short-term mission trips. According to Dusty Abel, Ralph's great grandson and a fifth generation Meloon, the company sponsors local and international service trips. "We are involved with Habitat for Humanity and giving food during holidays. In 2006, we took our first international mission trip to Mexico. We went to Tijuana to help build a home. Each employee pays $250 to go, and the company covers the rest of the cost. We offer one or two trips annually, depending on how many people want to participate. These trips are service centered, not necessarily evangelical."

In addition to deeply caring about their employees and serving others, the Meloons allowed Christian values to guide business decisions. Never was that more important than in 1957 when everything the company stood for was put to the test. Life was good when they received a large government contract that ushered in great expectations for the future. Unfortunately, it was not long before the inspectors made a veiled request for a payoff. They weren't even sure if they had heard him correctly, but within days the inspectors started finding "flaws" that were fatal to the boats. They considered just paying them off, but that would not be trusting God. Unfortunately, the story got worse. They had made the decision to try to satisfy the contract in spite of the situation, but they were losing significant money. Ultimately, they could not continue and filed for protection under bankruptcy laws. They met with creditors, and with their vote of confidence, the Meloons were allowed to repay their debts at ten cents on the dollar. Although not a requirement, they committed to repay all the debts in full. It took them until 1985, but they made good on that commitment. A dishonest inspector nearly destroyed them, but God took them through the fire, and it established their reputation for integrity.

If you were to meet Ralph, he would probably give you a business card. But his card is unique; it's double-sized and folded in half. On the inside, it reads:

Dear Friend, It has been a pleasure meeting you. May I share with you a little about our company and myself? Our family began building boats more than eighty years ago. We are one of the oldest boat manufacturing companies in the United States. We believe we manufacture one of the finest lines of recreational boats with inboard engines. They are owned and enjoyed by several Kings and Rulers in various nations. Nautique boats are used as official towboats in more than 80 percent of water ski and wakeboard tournaments around the world. Every one of our boats starts in a master mold. The craftsmen know how to put it all together and the raw materials soon turn out to be another quality boat. As a young man I discovered from the Bible that there is a Master Builder, God Himself. He can take a man's life, no matter how rough it seems to be, and create a new life that will be beautiful and useful. Life has been worth living since I asked Jesus Christ to become the Master Builder in my life and to recreate in me a new life, which would be pleasing to Him. He will do the same for you if you ask Him.

Please write me if I can be of help to you.

Sincerely,
Ralph C. Meloon, Sr.

Ralph's unwavering commitment to boldly integrate faith and vocation is a model for all of us. I can imagine the time when Ralph is ushered into heaven and hears those coveted words, "Well done, my faithful servant."[7]

7. This article is based on Merlin Switzer, *Bold Leadership* (Rocklin, CA: Public Policy Institute at William Jessup University, 2012) Kindle Edition. 508-535.

CHAPTER 6

WHAT IS OUR MARKET?

He said to them, "Go into all the world
and preach the gospel to all creation."

MARK 16:15 NIV

Ninety-eight percent of Christians worldwide are not in full-time ministry. These men and women spend the majority of their waking lives in work-related activity—whether at the office, networking off campus in community organizations, or simply spending time recreationally with friends. These Christians are frontline missionaries for Christ, yet most of them have never been trained for their mission.

James Davison Hunter echoes this problem when he said, "When the church does not provide the theologies that make sense of work and engagement in [the workplace], the church fails to fulfill the charge to 'go into all the world.'"[8] Jesus would have agreed. Much of His ministry was focused on work or the marketplace. Of his 132 public appearances, all but ten were in the marketplace. Forty-five of His fifty-two

8. James Davison Hunter, quoted from *To Change the World* on "Center for Paith & Work at LeTourneau University," http://centerforfaithandwork.comlabout/churchlwhy.

parables were set in the workplace.[9] None of his key leaders came from the religious establishment; they all left regular work responsibilities to serve alongside Christ. They weren't originally equipped to do ministry, but Jesus trained them. He started building his kingdom with these workplace disciples, and I believe it is our call to finish building what he started. But we first need to realize that without Him, we can do nothing (John 15:5). However, "I can do all things through Him who gives me strength" (Phil. 4:13 NIV).

This need in the marketplace is why FCCI is in the business of training leaders to run their companies for Christ. Our goal is for every business that is owned or run by a Christian leader to be run on biblical principles with a bottom line of leading people to the Lord (salvation), growing them up in the Lord (sanctification), and serving their fellow man (service). Our "market" is the entire world, and in all likelihood if we had total market penetration, it would mean that the Great Commission had been completed.

Very simply, our market is every workplace throughout the *world*! In Acts 1:8, Luke records Jesus' words, "You will be my witnesses in Jerusalem, and in all Judea and Samaria, and to the ends of the earth" (NIV). The model used at FCCI is to start in your city, move into your larger territory (states, provinces, etc.), and then grow internationally "to the ends of the earth." It starts next door, down the street, or around the corner. We must learn to walk alongside each other in fellowship, equipping and encouraging one other as we go along the way. Each company that joins this movement

9. "Why the Church Shouldn't Ignore the Workplace,"
The Center for Faith and Work at LeTourneau University,
http://centerforfaithandwork.comlaboutlchurchlwhy.

makes a significant impact on accomplishing our goal. Our mission is to change the world for Christ, one company at a time. One by one, we will ultimately gain a critical mass and change the communities in which we live. Transformation is the end game.

DISCOVERING TRANSFORMATION

George Otis is president of the Sentinel Group, a Christian research ministry that investigates the spiritual dynamics at work in cities and communities. Sentinel set out to determine if they could find any cities, worldwide, that were in a state of spiritual transformation, based on objective standards. They wanted to identify that the presence of God was influencing and changing *every* part of society in those places—legally, politically, economically, educationally, morally, ecologically, and spiritually—but that influence and change had to be measurable.

In 1995, Sentinel released *Transformations*, a video documentary that highlighted four such cities—Cali, Columbia; Almolonga, Guatemala; the Hebrides of Scotland; and the Eastern Arctic of Canada. These cities were declared to be in a place of spiritual transformation. These cities were shining brightly for the Lord. It was like the great revivals we're taught about in our schoolbooks, yet it was happening today. A number of years after this video was released, I had the opportunity to visit the mountain village of Almolonga, Guatemala, with a small group of peers. We sat and listened to the men God had used to lead this revival. They told of its beginning in prayer and how the idols were ripped out of the Catholic churches; how God closed the taverns and then the jails, because they had no need for them; and how He brought renewed prosperity to this small farming town. It was awesome. Instead of one harvest they had four, and the produce they reaped was super-sized. I held carrots that were the size of my forearm. The total harvest had increased fourfold.

People came from all over the world to learn from the farmers of Almolonga. The mayor freely gave away their secrets. He said he had *three great consultants* who provided all the answers to their questions: the Father, Son, and Holy Ghost! These three consultants moved through this village, and today Almolonga is ninety-three percent Christian.

The foundation of prayer was certainly a central and consistent part of the testimonies of the communities presented in *Transformations*. But I wondered what other factors might be instrumental in moving these communities in the direction of transformation. Commerce and business are significant aspects of city life, of course, but how significant could the role of business be in leading the transformation of other communities in the future?

COMMITMENT

Some ten years later, at a Transformations conference in Atlanta, I got a clear answer. Researchers had now found four hundred cities that were in a state of transformation, based on the same factors and methodology used in the 1995 study. One of these was a small town in England where Warren Sinclair ran a dot-com business. Warren shared a unique testimony of commitment in the way he ran his business for Christ.

Warren's business had struggled to survive the dot-com

crash, but it was still alive, hanging by a thread. The top managers were all Christians, and they wanted to honor the Lord through their business. They decided that with their depleted resources and lack of clear opportunities, prayer was the only answer. As a team, they each committed to rise every day at 5:00 a.m. to pray for two hours. Then, when they all arrived at the office at 8:00 a.m., they would pray together for another hour. Finally, a full-time, salaried prayer intercessor would lead individuals in prayer for another four hours each day. In fact, this intercessor carried the same salary as the CEO!

God honored their commitment to Him. To say this was a well-prayed-for company is a huge understatement. Some of the results were predictable. Their fortunes turned and the business prospered, but what was less predictable was that their commitment to prayer and honoring the Lord also changed the men and women who worked at this company. And what no one predicted was the way that commitment to prayer would spill over into the community. The city at large was so changed that it was included as one of Sentinel's "cities in transformation." This company was committed to honoring the Lord dramatically, and that transformed a small city in the lukewarm country of England. That's the impact of one company.

INTENTIONALITY

It is possible, in our enthusiasm to serve God, that we plan and strategize and even forecast ways to serve Him. We make our plans for His glory, but King Solomon reminds us, "The heart of man plans his way, but the Lord establishes his steps"

(Prov. 16:9 ESV). And the poet Robert Burns famously said, "The best laid schemes of mice and men go often awry."[10] Even our best attempts to glorify God can be flipped on their heads in favor of His better plan. God will always direct us to the "market" He wants us serving if we trust Him with all our hearts, lean not to our understanding, and acknowledge Him in all our ways (Proverbs 3:5-6).

When this happens, it may catch you by surprise, just like it did for me one day when I received an unexpected e-mail which read:

Dear Mr. Mitchell,

My name is Brave Yao. I am a Buddhist. I am a competitor, and I went on your website to learn about your products so I could take away all of your business. But I was so overwhelmed with your Christian commitment on your website that I want you to come to China and teach me about Jesus Christ.

Sincerely,
Brave Yao

Needless to say, I was overwhelmed, but I *did* go to China. I have been teaching Brave about Jesus, one small step at a time. I also bought a major stake in his business, and we have taught biblical character qualities (without Bible references) to the employees using the Character First materials. The Chinese government inspected and approved these materials and even asked us to expand our teaching to the whole province.

10. Translation of "To a Mouse," *Robert Burns, Robert Burns: Poems and Songs* (Dover: Mineola, NY: 1991) 32.

If my commitment to these purposes hadn't been intentional, I probably would have overlooked this letter as simply a bizarre competitor across the world and would have dismissed him. But instead through God's vision in my life, I was able to see that this was an opportunity to expand His kingdom into a place where very little light seems to shine for Christ. He brings us opportunities all the time, but we must have the eyes to see them. The problem that many warriors for the gospel struggle with is the question why is the world still so dark, if there are so many Christians in the world. One answer is that our light is not shining bright enough to dispel the darkness. But that may not be the whole story. A great flame grows from a tiny ember. It takes time for God's purposes to be accomplished. In some markets, we have to work for a very long time before we see any results. We must be patient in our intentionality; it just may be that it takes time for the light to grow. You may have to wait for a critical mass of Christ-honoring companies to develop before we can see an explosive move of the Spirit.

Light received brings more light, but light rejected brings darkness. God is not the problem, we are. When we are on the mountaintop and start to relax, we can slide into the valley. "A little sleep, a little slumber, a little folding of the hands to rest, and poverty will come upon you like a robber, and want like an armed man" (Proverbs 24:33–34 ESV). We must remain intentional in our purpose of taking the gospel to the world, or the light will certainly grow dimmer.

In addition to carrying the gospel forward, we must also regularly look back to be sure that we have built God-honoring businesses on good foundations. As Paul matured

as a leader and headed out on his third missionary journey, he
returned to the churches he had planted, "strengthening all
the disciples" (Acts 18:23 NIV). At the end of that journey,
he warned the Ephesian elders, "I know that as soon as I'm
gone, vicious wolves are going to show up and rip into this
flock . . . So stay awake and keep up your guard. Remember
those three years I kept at it with you, never letting up,
pouring my heart out with you, one after another" (Acts
29-31 MSG). Be sure you build your ministry on a solid
foundation and maintain it.

ALIGNMENT

Are we not committed enough to sustain a revival or to see
the Great Commission accomplished? If we don't shine bright
enough, how do we shine more brightly? If the vicious wolves
have started to tear in among our flock, how do we protect
them? These are difficult questions. And the answers aren't
necessarily easy either—especially for those God has equipped
as leaders, who are skilled at accomplishing goals and getting
things done. But here it is. God has to do the work through
us. We are just not capable of doing it ourselves. We must
have God's power running through us if we are going to
glorify Him.

Imagine a cylinder open at both ends and immersed in a
river. You're holding it down under the water, perpendicular
to the flow of the river. It is completely full of water, but
the water is not moving through the cylinder. It is stagnant.
However, if the cylinder is turned slightly so that it is partially
oriented to the flow, the water starts to move through the
cylinder very slowly. Finally, if, and only if, the cylinder is

perfectly aligned with the flow of the river, the maximum amount of water can flow through it.

Our lives are like this cylinder. If we accept Christ as our Savior, we are filled with His Spirit. We can never be more full of Christ than we are at that moment. Nevertheless, if we are not properly aligned to Him, we may not experience the fullness of His power. If we have perfect alignment, we have maximum flow.

How does this alignment occur? It happens through commitment to God's Word, intentionality in prayer, and watching for Him to work in the world around you. And it occurs by being aware of the opportunities He brings to you, not those that you plan for yourself. Ephesians 5 tells us that we are to be continually filled with the Spirit as in the example of the aligned cylinder and gives us wonderful, succinct advice on living a life aligned with God's purposes. "Be filled with the Spirit. Speak to one another with psalms, hymns, and spiritual songs. Sing and make music in your heart to the Lord, always giving thanks to God the Father for everything in the name of our Lord Jesus Christ. Submit to one another out of reverence for Christ" (5:18–21 NIV).

Clearly, the "market" is wide open, but it takes commitment, intentionality, and alignment with God's purposes to reach business leaders and have them join the movement of operating companies as platforms for ministry. Businesses come in all shapes and sizes, creating many different products and providing a variety of services. But if the Christian businessmen and -women in a given community operated their companies for Christ, they would transform their community.

The math is stunning. Each business of one hundred employees touches ten thousand people a year! That's customers, suppliers, competitors, families, and other business contacts. If companies truly had a focus on salvation, sanctification, and service, you could complete the Great Commission within a few short years. You could fund and mobilize an army of witnesses for Christ.

———

God is working in the marketplace. The Billy Graham organization did a study on various ministry opportunities they wanted to be involved with over the next fifty years. The marketplace was one of the top four. They wanted to test this marketplace ministry, so they pulled in several like-minded organizations to form a committee and discuss how to do that. The result was to put on four *His Presence in the Workplace* conferences in four different cities. Ron O'Guinn, who had headed up reconciliation for Promise Keepers, was on the committee with Jack Munday of the Billy Graham Training Center, Os Hillman of the International Coalition of Workplace Ministries (ICWM), and Kent Humphreys, President of FCCI at the time. Since FCCI is a ministry that is focused on building the kingdom of God by partnering with other like-minded ministries to accomplish that purpose, we were heavily involved in these conferences. I got to know Ron pretty well.

Ron was the pastor of a small church in Grapevine, Texas, and caught the vision of ministering to his community through the businesses there. He went into all the businesses in Grapevine asking how he could serve them. He started by asking if he could pray for them, but that quickly expanded into many other services such as performing marriages or funerals, counseling, giving devotionals, teaching Bible studies, and so on. It was a first-century-church model that I wanted to see in action, so I traveled to Texas and spent several days visiting the various businesses Ron touched. It was a great experience, and we became fast friends.

One of the businesses we visited was a relatively large acoustical systems business. We went in and Ron introduced me to the owner, Chris Jordan, and I told him about the ministry of FCCI; I explained that Chris was a "priest" and his company was his priesthood. We had an instant rapport and our conversation went on for the next hour; Ron was almost a spectator.

Chris was hurting. He was burned out by all of the jobs he had undertaken for his church; his business and marriage were experiencing difficulties; he felt worthless because he wasn't in full-time ministry. We shared our hearts with each other. I explained that we were all in full-time ministry and that God had him exactly where He wanted him. He needed to bloom in the marketplace by ministering to those around him. His company was his church and they needed him. He caught the vision instantly. His demeanor changed from near despair to excitement. This meeting was just a moment when one man shared with another, essentially about a call to the marketplace, and the other man heard that call. *Chris realized he was in full-time ministry!*

When I got home, I had a three-page email from Chris sharing his excitement and how my visit had saved his life. He was fired up and ready to go and be involved in this ministry.

It just took a moment. Today Chris is one of the great leaders of FCCI, with a booming Texas in front of him. As I finished the trip with Ron, I asked him what had been the most significant part of the trip for him. He acknowledged that we had many wonderful meetings, but he said that without question the most impactful was the meeting with Chris Jordan. He said that he realized that he couldn't meet Chris' needs, but that I could as a peer. He said, "Whenever I get in that situation again, I'll know what to do. I now have an FCCI arrow in my quiver that I can use whenever I need it."

KEY CONCEPTS

- The Great Commission can be accomplished through the marketplace, if we pray and are committed, intentional, and aligned with God!

- One company can make a difference.

- Light received brings more light, but light rejected brings darkness.

- Be sure to build your life and your business on a good foundation and maintain it.

- If we have perfect alignment with God, we have His maximum power flowing through us.

MARIAN NORONHA
Slaves as a Market

M arian Noronha is a passionate evangelist who was born in India, moved to the USA as a young man and worked his way through college. He became an expert in turbine technology and is the president of Turbocam International. Marian has developed a way of sharing the gospel that seemed very natural to him, just like telling a story:

> There's a guy who made some serious mistakes, and he ended up owing a million bucks. He had just a small amount of income, so there was no way he would ever pay off his debt. So, he thought he'd get a better job by taking some college courses. Although he's making $50,000 a year now, he's not even scratching the surface of the interest on this debt. Therefore, he heads to Alaska to work on a fishing boat or the pipeline . . . He plans to work his tail off and make some money. Now he's making $100,000, and he can finally tell his debtor that now he can at least start paying on the interest. But he thinks he can do better, so he starts working at a bar at night. Now he's making another $20,000 a year. But after a few weeks he gets sick, and he falls behind again. The best he can do is not good enough, but it's the best he can do. So one day he decides to talk to the guy he owes money to and explain to him that he's not really making headway, but he's trying really hard.

He calls him up and the guy says, "Listen, yesterday somebody came in, asked about you by name, and then he pulled out a check. He asked how much you owed and wrote a check to pay off everything that you owe me. So you are free, man."

So this guy walks out in a daze and he says, "My choices are that I'm a free man, and I'm going to have to start life as a free man, but I don't know how to do this. Or, you know what, maybe I'd better be careful. This could just be a silly story. I better not get my hopes up, because I'll have to get back to work tomorrow. Or, really, I've been working to pay this debt for so long that I haven't had a life. I should borrow $100,000 and do some things that I always wanted to do.

This became the method by which he introduced the gospel and told the story of how Jesus set him free. He had a debt that was way too big for him to be able to pay, but Jesus set him free. He didn't imagine how close he'd come to this story over the years that followed as he shared the gospel throughout southern Asia.

Marian found out about a man in the church in Bangalore, where he was speaking, who had just become a Christian, and he owed $10,000 in debt. His interest rate was high and he made a meager income. Marian thought that if he could pay off this man's debt, it would be a great opportunity to show what Jesus did for him. But before he could help the man, the man landed in prison for evading his debtors. Marian was sad and frustrated, but God revealed a new and bigger opportunity to him on his flight home. London's *Sunday Telegraph* had an article about slavery in Nepal. These families were living as slaves because they owed debts of around $400; for the same $10,000 he'd planned to spend on the one man who ran off, Marian could save twenty-five families from life as slaves in their debtor's prison.

When Marian got back home, he started doing his homework. He had an assistant dig up all the information she could and asked a friend in India to help do some research. A missionary in Nepal named Faye McDonald and a journalist named Gopal Sherma got on board too. They discovered that Nepal was one of those countries closed to the gospel. At the time, if anyone was baptized, they would get a three-year prison sentence; and anyone who baptized them would be given six years in prison. That was the law.

Nevertheless, in January 1999, Marian and Gopal went back to Nepal and bought seven families out of slavery.[11] The next year they went back and bought another thirty-five families, and they settled on a little less than eight acres of land that Marian had purchased for them to live on. By 2001, they had established three small villages on this land—Faith Town, Hope Town, and Love Town. About ninety-two families were eventually settled on this land.

Then, from about 2001-2006, Noronha was prevented from traveling to the country because of the Nepalese Civil War. But when he went back at the first opportunity in the fall of 2006, he found that a rudimentary school had been developed in one of the villages; the other two had no educa-

---

11. This story is told in Marian Noronha's movie *Captives*. You can find more info at www.captivesthefilm.com and www.bridgetonepal.blogspot.com

tion system. So he started an effort to build schools. Grace School was inaugurated in May 2008, and they now support six schools there and in nearby villages. Marian's assistant, Dawn Corbin, who originally helped him do research on this issue, —is now making her own trips to Nepal with her husband, John, and they are building orphanages with money they're raising in their hometown of Boston. Through these efforts they're eventually planning to start clinics, build wells, establish micro loans, grow livestock, create jobs, and so on. Marian, Dawn, Gopal, and Faye are touching the lives of five thousand people by modeling what Jesus did for us—not simply redeeming us but actually walking alongside us until we achieve the abundant life he offers us.

Marian's financial expertise took his ministry to more places than just those battling slavery and poverty in Nepal. While he was on a tour of India with FCCI leaders Bobby Mitchell, Cade Willis, and Kent Humphries, he found that he heard the same refrain from Christian business owners there over and over. "It's easy for you to tell us not to accept bribes, but how can we survive in an economy that's based on them? If we don't pay, we'll never make it in our businesses."

Marian got the idea to have these men band together and go public. By making a list of business owners who won't pay *or accept* bribes, they were able to create the No Bribe Coalition. They became a force that worked together, called on each other for support, and worked together politically to eradicate bribes from the market in Bangalore and Gora. People slowly became willing to try this new way of doing business.

Eventually they created a symbol for the No Bribe Coalition, and business owners in India now put it on their business cards and in storefronts so they can stand up and be counted among those who won't pay or accept bribes. As soon as they pull out their business cards, it becomes clear to the recipients that if they are going to be involved in bribery, then they can't do business.

Marian Noronha's journey has proven that once God gives you a vision, He'll equip you to follow through with it as long as you're willing to put in the effort. Instead of brushing the news of slavery in Nepal aside as a tragic side effect of a broken economic system, he was faithful to bring the goodness of God into that broken world and let His light grow there. Now thousands of people have been impacted by his faithfulness. You can do the same.

JOHN COORS
Investment vs. Charity

During one of John Coors' many trips to Africa, he looked out of his airplane's window and saw no light. The CEO of CoorsTek, the world's largest technical ceramics manufacturing company, knew many people lived on the ground below, but what he saw confirmed to him that they were living in darkness. He felt God was calling him to bring light—literally and metaphorically—to these people. He spent the next ten years working to provide modern lighting and cooking to the 500 million African people without access to electricity and for whom a wood fire was their sole means of cooking. This work was done as a charitable endeavor, and initially, by outward appearance the program was a success. It brought electricity and propane stoves to more than 100,000 people who had been living in the "Dark Ages." But Coors says, "It's a tragic story of misunderstanding God's call, which was to help these people but not from the foundation of a non-profit platform. All those I thought I had helped are now back where they started and have had their hopes dashed again."

Coors says, "I consider people stuck in grinding poverty to be captives. Our charity brought light and some basic conveniences to thousands of people, but what will truly free them from this bondage and suffering are jobs. Here, too, I have witnessed firsthand that charity is not the answer. For many years I have supported children's homes in Kenya, where we have clothed, fed, educated and trained hundreds of children with a mission to provide them with a productive future. What we have succeeded in doing is building false hopes among these decent people, for there are no jobs for them upon entering adulthood. This experience exposed to me the true limits of charity."

Charity cannot create the jobs that will lead to economic freedom for the millions of people so enslaved. It's the right tool for certain things but not for economic development. It's like trying to tighten a bolt with a hammer. A lesson I, and many others, have learned the hard way is that employing philanthropy in this way actually makes the problem worse by creating dependency, which sustains poverty. This is now widely understood, but I wish I had known it ten years ago."

Coors is a founding member of a values-based private investment movement called, One Thousand & One Voices, involving influential families investing relational, intellectual and patient financial capital to provide a pathway to economic freedom in developing markets, starting in Africa. He says: "*One Thousand & One Voices* was established with the belief that the pathway to economic freedom – real prosperity for millions living in poverty – is through values-based private investment grounded in the time-tested principles of free enterprise."

His message to FCCI and Christian business leaders around the world would be, "Don't try to fix the world using any tools other than the ones we know work already. FCCI members are all successful business people and your three-dimensional capital – your intellectual, relational, and patient financial capital – is what's needed to build and grow successful companies that will provide jobs." Ironically, the world seems to be suggesting that profit is evil and nonprofit is good when it comes to helping people in developing markets. "Even the church is sending a message to businessmen that making money is somehow not part of God's best and that you can do more good through non-profit work. If we want economic recovery and growth, we need to utilize all of the talents and assets of those who have already created jobs and prosperity in many areas of the world – people who have built profitable, successful businesses."

John Coors has a passion to help business people understand that doing business is in and of itself a holy calling. It's good in all of its aspects, and we don't have to be embarrassed about it. Simple wealth transfer will never create wealth for people living in poverty; the only thing that creates wealth is investment. "My heart breaks for the 600 million people in sub-Saharan Africa who still cook with wood fires. They can't get medical care. They can't get anything. And we're trying to fix it with wealth transfer. It will guarantee they will be impoverished forever."

Coors insists that the only thing that will work is to create jobs. It's so simple. What people really need is a job that they're proud of and that pays at a level that can bring economic freedom for themselves and their families. And the only way these kinds of jobs are created is through successful businesses. That's where FCCI comes in. We need legitimate investment, and we're expecting returns. We can apply the parable of the minas where Jesus said, "Go and do business." That's what we're supposed to be doing. It's a holy calling, and it lifts people out of poverty into the middle class and gives people a hope and a future.

One Thousand & One Voices is making this happen through a $300 million investment fund dedicated to developing small and medium businesses in Africa. When people start having jobs, then they start having some money, and they use that money to buy goods and services, which creates more opportunities. It's a wonderful cycle.

Coors says, "You know, my great-grandfather was a penniless orphan immigrant to the U.S. Through loans from visionary investors, he was able to create a brand that's become a household name. What a wonderful thing he was able to do. I would like to see people all over the world have that same kind of opportunity."

CHAPTER 7

WHAT'S IN THE TOOLBOX?

> "And my God shall supply all your needs
> according to his riches in glory in Christ Jesus."
> PHILLIPIANS 4:19 NASB

"Well done, good and faithful servant: thou hast been faithful over a few things, I will set thee over many things; enter thou into the joy of thy Lord." (Matt. 25:21 ASV) is what we all want to hear when we finish life's race. We want to finish strong and make our lives count. All Christians want that, but not all Christians are businessmen and not all of them are called to operate their companies for Christ. However, all Christians (teachers, housewives, administrators, employees, accountants, athletes, actors, care givers, and so on) are called to manage what God has entrusted them with, just as the faithful servant in the parable of the talents did.

We've learned that the market is everywhere there is a business, whether it's next door or halfway around the world. But the bigger issue is, how you transform a secular business into one that honors God and is used as a platform for ministry? What are the tools that can facilitate that transformation and sustain a company while it's being run for Christ?

We need tools for any size event: masses (100,000-plus), conferences (500), groups (12), council of advisors (3), or personal study or sharing (1). That's the pattern Jesus used, so it should still work for us today. Remember that life change occurs in small groups and intimacy with a few (Peter, James, and John).

COMMITTED LEADERSHIP

For a Christian businessman in a position to guide and direct a company, it all starts from the belief that God owns it all, and he must manage the various assets of the company (people, equipment, processes, relationships, customers, knowledge, money, giving, and so on) in such a way as to build the kingdom of God and operate a company for Christ. The key is committed leadership. The CEO, business owner, and primary leaders must be deeply committed to operating a company for Christ. It is essential that they understand that they are God's companies, and they need to manage them for His glory, not theirs. They must be intentional and focused on completing the task. Without the absolute commitment of a company's decision makers, *it cannot be run as a company for Christ*. This is the one essential step in the transformation of a company from secular to sacred. No tool in the toolbox can overcome this.

FCCI CONFERENCES AND TRAINING

However, the other tools in the toolbox can greatly facilitate this transformation if the leadership has this incredibly deep commitment level. The Fellowship of Companies for Christ is all about equipping and encouraging CEOs, business owners, and company leaders personally in and through their businesses in such a way as to accomplish Christ's eternal objectives as set forth in the Bible. It's a difficult journey, but FCCI can be a great help along the way. Our members have created many, many tools and have shared them with others. Moses' shepherd's crook became the tool of his calling. Cast down, it became a serpent; taken up in faith, it became the rod of God. Some tools are unique and others commonplace, but the primary ones FCCI uses are as follows:

- Conferences
- Groups
- Materials
- Prayer
- Testimonies
- Technology
- Partnerships

In 1980, we started as a conference ministry, similar to a trade association. We were small businessmen with virtually no experience running a ministry, much less one with very limited resources and dependent on volunteers. But what was evident in 1980 was that there was a hunger for fellowship and a desire to find out how others were trying to operate a "Christian company." Some people had been on the journey for a while and were thrilled to find out they weren't alone. Others were just starting down that path with our limited guidance, but they now had connections to approximately one hundred CEOs or business owners trying to honor God through their businesses. It was no longer so lonely at the top. Much sharing, counsel, discussions, and advice happened at the conferences and in between. It met a need and fellowship flourished.

As the Fellowship of Companies for Christ began to emerge, conferences were clearly the primary tool in our toolbox. Maybe the only tool, but others quickly evolved into a number of secondary ones. Conferences were and still are the most effective way to cast a vision for the ministry and build our membership base. They also serve as the "town hall meeting place," where our members gather to renew relationships and enjoy great fellowship. From those very early days, the sharing of our stories, our *testimonies*, was eagerly sought by all, and it allowed us to learn from actual experiences. We often set up show-and-tell tables where our members could show how they'd stamped Bible verses in the bottom of pie pans or included tracts with every shipment their company sent out. In a real way, we became models and examples for each other. Hundreds of testimonies have been shared over the years, and they continue to be an effective and efficient way to communicate the message.

Initially, we thought conferences were primarily about teaching, and then we realized the power of fellowship, which became the unique aspect of our conferences. The thought of operating a company as a platform for ministry was almost unknown at the time, and there were virtually no materials written on the subject. The conference teaching was constantly plowing new ground. It was fresh and new every day. When a committed and searching businessman was first exposed to the concept of "companies for Christ," he instantly grasped the vision and his life was changed forever. You could see it in his eyes. It became *his vision*, and he pursued it with vigor! That same transformation of the heart continues to happen today when someone grasps the vision for the first time. Thirty-three years ago it was a brand new thought, but even today only a small percentage of Christian businessmen have ever been exposed to this teaching. That's the challenge, but now, new technology will allow us to reach the world.

FCCI is world renowned for the excellence of its conferences. They've been held at world-class facilities, with top-notch speakers and are known for building wonderful relationships and having incomparable fellowship. The quality of the teaching is critical. It is difficult to get speakers to create new messages for the FCCI conferences rather than using canned messages that they typically give multiple times each year, but we knew it was critical for us to have material specifically developed for our members. In the beginning, it would have been an impossible task had it not been for the early commitment of Bruce Wilkinson, Larry Burkett, Walt Wiley, and Ron Blue. They carried the conferences for the first few years, particularly Bruce and Larry. Early conferences had Bruce or Larry speaking three or four times, supported by other speakers and businessmen with compelling testimonies, such as Stanley Tam and Truett Cathy. We also had panels and group discussions. We were small and resource challenged, but excellence was our trademark.

It became evident that attendees wanted more. They wanted to get together between conferences, either at smaller conferences, through small groups, or via first-class training materials that were transferrable. After repeated requests, the board recognized that there was a hunger in the membership that had to be addressed. In the early 1980s, the executive committee developed a blueprint for the growth of the ministry. Bottom line, we decided to build staff, produce materials, and test small groups.

The materials we produced included case histories, testimonies, focus cards, and audio and videotapes of all conference sessions, packaged in such a way that they would be easy to use in teaching sessions within our own companies or in group settings with other members who were unable to attend the conferences. In those days only CEOs or business owners and their spouses could attend the conferences, because we wanted to provide a secure environment for private discussions or counsel. So audio- or videotapes became the only way company executives could be exposed to this training. It took another fifteen years before we decided to reverse that policy and expand the ministry to include key company leaders. We decided we would "test" the concept of a small group, but in reality the use of the materials had already initiated the small group concept before we officially introduced it. God moved miraculously in many areas of the ministry, and this was just one more case where He guided and directed us.

We introduced our "test" fellowship group on April 13, 1982, and called it "The Atlanta Chapter." It met on the second Tuesday of each month from seven to nine o'clock in the morning. We did not have a rigid structure, but the format was:

7:00–7:20 a.m.
   fellowship over coffee and breakfast pastries

7:20–7:50 a.m.
   listen to teaching via audio- or videotape
   or hear a testimony

7:50–8:30 a.m.—
   discuss the impact of the teaching
   on our businesses

8:30–9:00 a.m.
   close with focused prayer for our families,
   employees, businesses, FCC members,
   and so on.

This model was very successful and was used in the developing chapters or "local fellowship groups." Today, these are called "business leadership groups" and are spreading around the world. Members are studying materials on more than one hundred topics in five languages.[12]

WILLINGNESS TO SACRIFICE

God used Moses' crook as a tool. He can use anything. Sometimes the tool He uses can be a telephone, jet plane, hotel room, or meal, and the result can be much fruit. Early in the life of FCC, I got a strange call from Tiberias, Israel. It was from Ken Crowell, President of Galtronics, who had heard of FCC. He said, "I understand that you know how to run a Christian business." I replied that I didn't know how to run a company for Christ, but that we had a fellowship of

12. There are other groups that meet the needs of special situations, but
    we will discuss those in more detail in chapter 8: What is a Group?

companies that were trying to learn how to do that. He asked if he could come to Atlanta and meet with the leadership of FCC to try to understand our journey. Ken came, and we met for several days. He told us about Galtronics, and we showed him what we were doing and answered his questions as best we could. His eyes showed that he clearly understood the vision and now owned it. Ken was a great friend and long-term member, attending many conferences until his recent death.

I had never heard the term *BAM* or *business as missions* until I met him. He was an expert in antenna technology and ultimately built Galtronics into a great global business with multiple sites worldwide. These were all significant businesses with the primary objective being to use them to operate with such excellence that they could earn the right to be heard and lead people to Christ. Ken was a pioneer wanting to use his business as a mission. Businesses can often go into countries that are blocked to the gospel if they have a legitimate business purpose. Ken had nearly a thousand employees in Israel and wanted to be a good corporate citizen, a blessing to Israel, *and* lead people to Christ. Several years ago, Galtronics received the coveted Kaplan Award for excellence in Israeli Industry. He was honored by the Knesset and featured on the front page of the newspaper under the headline "Galtronics, A Blessing to Israel". "All things are possible to him that believeth" (Mark 9:23 ASV).

But Ken's story does not end there. He developed a credit-card size digital audio player that presented the gospel message clearly and articulately. He later developed a slightly larger, solar-powered version, about the size of a smart phone, that contained the entire Bible and was available in over 4,600 languages and dialects. He named it MegaVoice and made it available to numerous Christian ministries to distribute to the billions of people worldwide who aren't able to read Scripture themselves. It was his desire that MegaVoice be perpetuated, so he worked with National Christian Foundation (NCF) to insure that it would go forward long after his death. Thousands and thousands of people have been saved and taught because of Ken's creativity and generosity, and many more will be in the future.

Not too long ago, Ken came to Atlanta to discuss some details with NCF for this ownership transfer, and we had a wonderful time of sharing at lunch. He asked me if I remembered the time many years before when he came to Atlanta in his quest to find out how to run a company for Christ, and I said that I did. He said that it had cost him a couple thousand dollars to come over here, and that was all the money he'd had at the time. I was shocked, but then he added that the money it cost him to come was the best money he ever spent. The cost of a telephone call, plane ticket, hotel room, and meals didn't cost FCC anything, but in the hands of the Master, they were great tools that have produced much fruit.

PARTNERSHIPS

The founders of FCCI were clear on our call and the mission and vision of the ministry, but we didn't understand how it would all come about. We had foundational operational concepts, such as the idea that the way you handle money is an outward indicator of an inward heart condition. We were committed never to be a begging ministry, to always operate within our means, and to never prevent someone from participating in FCC because of a lack of money. We acknowledged, with perfect unity, that this ministry belongs to God and that we hold it with an open hand, not to build turf for our kingdom, but to build the kingdom of God. Close working relationships or partnerships with other ministries to further the kingdom are also part of our DNA. For example, we've had a very close working relationship with National Christian Foundation (NCF) since its inception. We're able to draw on their financial, giving, and tax expertise to help our members, such as Ken Crowell structure a long-term solution for MegaVoice. Many of our members have their own accounts with NCF and have used NCF's advice to sell companies or multiply their ability to give. It's been a wonderful partnership for all concerned and is absolutely a tool in our toolbox. We also have partnership relationships with a number of other ministries including, Crown Financial Ministries, Walk Thru the Bible, Europartners, and Connection (CBMC), to name a few.

PRAYER

Prayer is the foundation of FCCI and a tool! We have an active prayer ministry, led by Bill Moeny, in which we regularly pray for the needs of the ministry, the member businesses, our people and their families, and other requests that are on the hearts of those who touch us. People can call in and add their requests to our prayer list. Every business leadership group has time set aside for prayer at each meeting. The board of directors and their wives regularly pray. The office staff prays daily. There is much prayer going on all over the ministry, and we are seeing miraculous answers. We understand that apart from God, we can do nothing. The journey we've been on is impossible apart from God's enabling. There is a long history of seeking God and turning any residual ownership that we stubbornly cling to over to him. We've encouraged our people to turn everything over to him. Many of our members have turned their businesses over to him in a formal way, through a consecration or dedication service. We've had several members put six-foot high crosses on their buildings. We are a praying people. These verses come to mind: "Those who seek me early will find me" (Prov. 8:17 KJV), and "The blessing of the Lord, it maketh rich, and he addeth no sorrow with it" (Prov. 10:22 KJV).

One morning I got an early call, advising that we'd had a fire at our plant the night before. From the phone call, it was not clear to me how much damage we had sustained or any of the details. When I got to the plant, I immediately saw that it had been a significant fire, and we had sustained considerable damage. The last employee left the plant in good shape the previous night at approximately ten thirty, and the first employees arrived the next morning at six o'clock to find the plant filled with smoke. In between, we had a significant fire resulting from multiple lightning strikes. The fire was extremely hot and widespread. We have a PVC cooling pipe running to several pieces of equipment in the vicinity of the fire. The pipe melted and water rushed out and put out the fire. Smoke was in the building, but the fire was out when our first employees arrived that morning.

The fire department had not been called, because no one was there when the fire was raging. If the fire had gone on even a few more minutes, several fifty-five-gallon barrels of oil would have exploded, and the entire building, including millions of dollars of equipment and all of our records, would have been destroyed. The damage to the business would have been irreparable. As it was, we sustained virtually no damage to any major equipment and were able to get back to production within days. All of the repairs took several months, but we were able to continue to serve our customers and maintain our business, and insurance covered all of our costs, even lost profit.

When I looked at the magnitude of the problem, I found it almost impossible to believe that a small water line could put out a raging fire with no assistance from anyone. I was overwhelmed with gratitude. I believe Satan attacked and God thwarted the attack. We serve a great God who blesses us even when we are asleep and who fights our battles for us. After all, it was his building that he was preserving. We had given it to him long ago.

KEY CONCEPTS

- A company cannot be run for Christ without the absolute commitment of the decision makers.

- We all need tools to help us along the way, but God can use anything, even a shepherd's crook.

- When someone grasps the FCCI vision, their life is changed forever. You can see it in their eyes!

- God blesses us even when we are asleep, and He fights our battles for us.

- "He is no fool who gives what he cannot keep to gain what he cannot lose." -Jim Elliot

WALT WILEY
Why FCCI Is Critical?

How did you get involved with FCCI as the MC?

In the early days of FCCI, they needed somebody to come for just ten or fifteen minutes to bring a devotional to get [their meetings] started. They asked me if I was willing to do that, so I went down there and gave them a devotional. Then, the next time they met, they said, "Hey, can you come and do that again?" When they planned their first conference they asked me to come to that as well, so I was there for the very first conference they ever had. Bruce [Wilkinson] and I did a lot of teaching at the conferences together. I used to always tell Bert [Stumberg] that if you have a conference like this, you need an MC, a face person who keeps order. When the next speaker gets up there, they know they're going to be instructed what to do next. And he said, "Yeah yeah."

Bert used to do it, and Bert was a great guy, but he was not an upfront guy. It wasn't his thing. He would jingle his change in his pocket while he talked to you. Anyway, I returned again and again to be a speaker, and finally Ray Miller, who became the president later, had this idea that what they needed was an MC. Well, who could do that? It's sort of my personality to be that kind of a person, and I usually do a lot of humor, so they asked me to MC it and then kept asking me back.

What impact has FCCI had on you and your company?

FCCI has had the greatest impact on my life in the area of encouragement and rubbing shoulders with men and women who are not in ministry, but in business. They see a bigger picture. I see men and women who say, "You know what? I'm not just going to use this business to make money. I'm going to use this as a ministry to impact people's lives for Christ." I tremendously admire them for that. FCCI has opened my eyes to the fact that one of the greatest ways to reach our society for Christ is through marketplace ministry.

I was speaking in Toronto to the leadership of Christian Businessman's Committee and FCCI in Canada. Another speaker at one of the sessions asked the audience when was the last time their church called people forward and said, "These are the Johnsons. They're heading out to Papua New Guinea next week, and we brought them up here to put hands on them, encircle them, and just commit them to God in prayer." You know, everybody responded, "Oh yeah, I've seen that in my church." Then he said, "When's the last time your pastor said, 'All you folks who tomorrow morning are going to be in some office working in some kind of a business, we're going to ask all of you to come forward. We're going to pray for you and ask God to use you in the marketplace.'" Of course his point was that we don't do that. We have sitting before us people who every day are walking into a place where there's an opportunity for a ministry, and we ought to be encouraging them and praying for them. I believe in that. That really opened my eyes.

What do you think is the most important take away from an FCCI conference?
I'm always glad I made the effort to go to the conferences, because they are a time of refreshment and re-energizing.

These international conferences are designed as a chance for people to get away. They're also designed to share ideas. A lot of business owners are in survival mode, and they're looking for suggestions and ideas from people who walk in the same shoes. And so whether it's from the front of the meeting room or from coffee breaks, shared meals, or sitting around the pool together, there's a constant sharing of ideas.

What makes FCCI different is that these are Christian CEOs who want to honor the Lord through business. They want to have an impact on their employees and vendors. And when they come to a conference like this, they hear how other people are doing that and they think, *Oohh, that's a good idea. I'm going to implement that.* I'm sure a lot of these people return from their conferences and they initiate some idea they gleaned.

I remember there was a man who was a regular attendee at the conference, and his four sons worked for him. They used to say to me that all of a sudden their dad would call an emergency meeting. He'd beckon for them to quickly drop everything and come to the room. They'd walk into the room and he'd say, "We're going to change this. We're gonna start doing this. We're going to get rid of that. We're going to implement this." And one of the sons said to me, "We would just sort of roll our eyes and say, 'Oh, guess what? Dad went to one of those conferences.'" So there's an encouragement [at the conferences] to do that.

Another thing is friendships. FCCI has helped form a lot of deep friendships. You'll see people sitting together informally, having coffee together, sitting around the pool, or having meals together, because individuals whom they call good friends today are people they met at an FCCI conference. Deciding to run your own business is a large, risky decision. Business owners are a different breed. They've got their own set of issues and challenges. A lot of their sons or daughters are at these conferences, and those kids have got their own set of baggage. They've got certain advantages. Why? Because their dad ran the business or their mom has a business. But there are a lot of challenges that come with that. The sons of Truett Cathy are friends of mine, and Dan and Bubba have benefited from their dad starting a restaurant called Chik-fil-A. But that also brought special challenges into their lives, because their dad owns a business. This conference brings these people together and allows them to see they're not alone. The guy sitting next to me is going through exactly what I'm going through. And when you're going through challenges, there's something encouraging in sharing those challenges. It doesn't necessarily help me, but it makes me feel better.

It is not only encouraging, but it's also challenging. Starting and conducting and surviving the challenges of running a company isn't an easy task. These people are not only trying to run a business and survive; they've increased their challenges and the difficulties by trying to run their business as a company for Christ. They've opened up Pandora's box to all kinds of problems. It's easy to drift away from that ministry side into just the business side. So when you come back to these meetings, there's a constant reminder to continue in ministry mode.

I think the conference provides prayer support in a lot of people's lives. These conferences and the friendships that have been formed invite regular contact between parties throughout the other months of the year. It opens doors for people to begin praying for one another, to be concerned about one another, and to share their personal lives. It goes beyond just the business side. It's personal. And all this happened because you came to a conference, and you met somebody else who shares your same vision.

CHAPTER 8
WHAT IS A GROUP?

> "For where two or three are gathered
> in my name, there I am among them."
> MATTHEW 18:20 ESV

What is a group? It sounds like a silly question, but it's really not. As we get into the details, we'll see how complicated it really is, but for now, let's go back to the question itself. Webster's Dictionary says a group is "an assemblage of objects regarded as a unit."[13] In FCCI terms, a group is two or more CEOs, business owners, or company leaders who meet for the purpose of equipping and encouraging one another as they seek to honor the Lord through their businesses. It is truly unique. They are related to each other by their purpose, their desire to follow Christ, love, and the camaraderie of the journey that bonds them to each other. Christ said that, "By this all men will know that you are my disciples, if you have love for one another" (John 13:35 NASB), and this is truly the mark of an FCCI group.

13. *Merriam-Webster's Collegiate Dictionary*, s.v. "group," accessed May 17, 2013, http://www.merriam-webster.comldictionarvlgroup

COUNCIL OF ADVISORS

There are many types of groups within FCCI. A "council of advisors" is a small accountability group of two or three, focusing on intimacy and speaking the truth into each other's lives. It is safe and secure and sometimes requires tough love. It is like having your own personal board of directors to speak wise counsel into your life and the life of your company, and then you are able to reciprocate to the other group members. You laugh, cry, and rejoice together. It's not so much about using the FCCI teaching materials; it's about helping your brother, picking him up when he is down, tending to his wounds, and being there when one needs a friend. It's probably the simplest FCCI group, but it is mighty in results. Remember, life change occurs in small groups.

Leonard Isaacs is from Beulah Land. That's the heartland of the land known as Middle Tennessee. He was a regional director of FCCI many years ago, but if you called him today his phone message would greet you by welcoming you to FCCI Beulah Land. I laughed when I heard the recording and asked him about it. He quickly advised that in his heart, he would be part of FCCI Beulah Land until he departed planet Earth. Leonard is a country storyteller par excellence. He can spin a yarn or tell some jokes, but his heart is in the marketplace. It is his great desire to lead businessmen to Christ and walk with them along the journey. He particularly liked the "counsel of advisors" tool and set up hundreds of counsels across Beulah Land. He was the great builder of these groups that have impacted so many, so deeply.

Nine days after the horrible tragedy of the 9/11 attacks, we stayed the course and held our planned International

Conference in Maui, Hawaii. Our attendance dropped from 560 to 350, and many other conferences were cancelled, so most people didn't know whether to go or stay home. I was happy to see Leonard's familiar face there, and he was tapped to give the closing comments at the end of the conference. This was one of, if not *the* greatest conference we ever had, in part because the attendees were so tender after our recent national tragedy, and in part because the primary speaker, Henry Blackaby, took us so deep. It was a God moment.

Leonard Isaacs closed the conference, stepped down from the podium, walked into the hallway, and promptly fell over with a massive heart attack. The Ritz was the only hotel on the island with defibrillators and a staff who knew how to use them. And use them they did. It saved his life and they were able to get him to the Island hospital, where the specialist he needed was a practicing surgeon named Mark Schwab. As he prepared to operate, Leonard asked him what his life was like before he became a committed Christian? The doctor stammered, but Leonard seized the opportunity and led him to saving faith in Christ in the next few minutes. Prior to the surgery, Dr. Schwab prayed out loud for the first time in his life. Leonard survived and spent the next two weeks at the condo of an FCCI friend, whose timeshare just happened to be for those two weeks. Leonard's story covered the entire front page of the Maui newspaper, plus more; it was a much better story than that of the previous week, when headlines announced that ten thousand people had lost their jobs.

God has a plan! I believe he does. There are no coincidences in the life of a Christian. This story started out to be about groups, but it moved to God's faithfulness, then prayer, and finally the revelation of his plan. And this is what His groups are all about. Jesus tells us to, "Let your light so shine before men, that they may see your good works, and glorify your Father which is in heaven" (Matt. 5:16 KJV).

Most members of FCCI think of the founders as the first small group of the ministry, but that's not actually the case. In the very early days prior to the beginning of FCC, several of us were hungry for information and would travel and network with others in our pursuit of God's call to the marketplace. Our search led to many places scattered around North America, but one of the most unusual trips was when four of us traveled to Owen Sound in northern Canada to attend the International Conference of Ambassadors for Christ. It was truly life changing. We went up there to see if these indigenous missionaries were worthy of our donations. The unexpected result was that we were transformed by the stories and prayers of these godly men who told us of their walk through the jungles, fights with witch doctors, and healing the sick. When we stood by these committed warriors, we paled in comparison. We were humbled by our pride and ego. We were ashamed, but then we knew what an authentic Christian looked like, and we had missionary models to emulate in the marketplace. God had to strip us of our pride, if we were going to build companies for Christ. We thought we were going as successful businessmen to give of our spoils, but we were confronted by people who had given everything. God continued the unexpected when we were told in a casual conversation about a man we ought to talk to if we really wanted to follow in His steps in the marketplace. His name was Fred Roach. He was from Texas, and God wanted him to teach us about groups and giving.

Fred was the largest homebuilder in North America, but he was very approachable and unassuming. In the world's eyes, he had an almost unbelievable income. But what no one really knew was that he gave virtually all of it away. His one indulgence was a cabin he owned in Hendersonville, North Carolina. After we returned from Canada and had a number of phone calls with Fred, he invited us to his mountain retreat for the weekend.

We arrived on a Friday afternoon and left after lunch on Sunday. In between, we had camaraderie, fellowship, teaching, learning, sharing, questioning, and laughing. We audiotaped the entire weekend, and we showed the first video we had ever produced. It highlighted Days Inn, Mrs. Kinzer's Foods, Applied Ceramics, and Central Atlanta Parking, and it told their testimonies. The weekend was a power-packed, energized gathering. It looked a lot like a conference, and was probably the first mini-conference, but in reality it was a fellowship group. In fact, it was the very first small group. It lasted a mere twenty to twenty-five hours, but it made a lasting impact. The type of fellowship group that Fred "showed" us evolved into what we now call a Business Leadership Group, which is our most widely used group and has ten to twelve participants that meet every other week.

The highlight of the weekend was Fred's story. He built homes. Lots of homes. More than anybody else in America, and he made lots of money. In the mid-1970s, a seven-figure income was absolutely the American Dream. Only that wasn't Fred's dream. He wanted to honor the Lord with the fruit of his labors. All of it! In those days, he kept $25,000 a year to live on and gave away the rest. He kept $5,000 in reserve and owned the cabin we were meeting in. He didn't even have a dishwasher in the cabin. We all have different calls and gifts. Fred's unique gift was to consistently give away more than ninety percent of his income. We discussed his personal finances in detail. We asked questions and even debated certain topics. I was mildly irritated that he included some secular organizations in his giving. At this point, it was still a few years before the SSS principle was even a thought, much less a guiding one. He gently shared that we need to help those in need around us, not just Christians or Christian causes. Fred was ahead of the curve. His gifts were for salvation and sanctification and service. "God loves a cheerful giver" (2 Cor. 9:7 NIV), and Fred was certainly that.

Fred shared a story about feeling guilty that he had not given generously to his wife. So one day he decided to give her a $5,000 diamond bracelet for a present. She *oohed* and *aahed* over the gift and wore it with pride. But one day not long afterwards, she came to him and said although she really loved and appreciated the bracelet, she would like to sell it and give the money to a particular ministry that God had laid on her heart! Fred and his wife were one in their call to give.

By the way, our group wanted to give Fred a nice gift in thanks for a phenomenal experience at his mountain retreat. We decided to give him a dishwasher, because we knew if we gave him money, he would only give it away. We had to make him promise not to sell it. We went to Canada to give, but God taught us what real commitment was all about and what it means to give everything. God gave us models of commitment and giving, even though they weren't on our agenda.

Councils of advisors (COAs) are typically composed of three people and don't require outside leadership. They are intimate and relatively easy to establish at low cost. Guidelines are available to help members get a COA started. They are very focused on the needs of the participants, and they bring high levels of accountability. Providing advice or counsel on specific issues is a great strength of COAs. They can be extremely effective, but they are not focused on teaching other than what occurs relationally or experientially. Business Leadership Groups (BLG) have all the elements of a COA, but they are much larger and have a strong emphasis on teaching. They don't have a paid facilitator, but they do have trained group leaders. There is wisdom in many counselors, and the additional people expand the business experiences and the ability to share. Most of our members will ultimately transition into a BLG, and these groups may last for many years. We believe that every member of FCCI should be in one of our groups, whether it's a COA, BLG, or CBO (see below). Many of our people transition from one type of group to another as their needs change. In my particular case, I was involved in two COA groups before we even labeled these groups as COAs. They met different needs. One involved an extensive prayer ministry and the charting of prayers and their answers. The other focused on our businesses and how to more effectively use them for the Lord. Both had extraordinary impact on my life, but my personal need for teaching, training, and equipping meant that I needed to be involved in a different type of group. So I joined a facilitated group know as a Christian Business Owner group or CBO.

FACILITATED GROUPS

Facilitated groups are very different from COA groups. I had been involved in one COA for approximately three years and the other for almost ten years, but I needed more help in running a business with excellence and bearing the maximum amount of kingdom fruit from our business. Typically a facilitated group is made up of leaders of eight to twelve larger companies. They are more difficult to put together and they're expensive, but they are very focused on meeting your needs on a deeper level. It's a safe place to get objective counsel from multiple sources. The advice can be brutal, no holds barred. It's advice without an agenda. Total accountability is painful. The key to a facilitated group is the quality of the leader.

CHRISTIAN BUSINESS OWNER GROUPS

I was in a Christian Business Owner (CBO) group for sixteen years. It was one of the great experiences of my life. We had an absolutely wonderful leader in Ted Sprague. He was responsible for organizing the program, arranging for the food, and securing the location. In addition, Ted was a great teacher and evangelist, but more importantly in this role, he had the ability to stimulate the conversation and not dominate it. He was invisible as a facilitator, one of us, not domineering. Our group changed significantly over time to meet our changing needs. Originally, we met for one full day a month. We would have a light breakfast, followed by an outside speaker, then lunch. Afterward, we would discuss the topic of the day or address specific issues we were dealing with in our personal or business lives. No subject was taboo. We were free to ask or discuss anything, but it had to stay in the room. We were bonded from the first meeting, and we had total freedom and access. It pushed the envelope downstream and made us accountable. If there was ever a time when I felt like I was doing what Jesus would do, it was during these years. These are men I went on missionary journeys with, shared my life with, and fellowshipped with. There's one word to describe this dynamic—*rich*!

The structure changed to two half-days a month, which was my favorite format. One day we would go into one of our member's operations, get a tour and presentation on company policies, followed by a look at the critical issues they were facing and soliciting input or suggested solutions from our members. It was energizing and stimulated thought among all of us. Ted used to say that this is the body of Christ at work. Likeminded brothers with a Christian worldview were drawing on years of experience, giving unfettered counsel to advance the company

As times changed and we became geographically diverse, the structure also had to change again. We moved to quarterly retreats to allow people to travel from long distances. It was more difficult, but the relationships didn't change. Ultimately we stopped meeting as a group on a regular basis, but we still have periodic reunions and the spirit is always sweet and the fellowship strong.

One of the tools that we have in our toolbox is our relationships or partnerships with like-minded ministries. We talked about National Christian Foundation and mentioned others, including Walk Thru the Bible. Several years ago, when Chip Ingram had just taken over as President of Walk Thru the Bible, they asked me to come to their President's Council in Boca Raton and open their conference by sharing about their partnership of many years with FCCI. I was happy to do that and shared who FCCI was and how we had partnered together over a number of years. I finished my talk and stepped down and looked forward to enjoying the conference. I had no expectations, but an unexpected and very interesting thing happened.

During the course of the conference, about fifteen or twenty people came up to me and said they had been involved with FCCI, and they commented, "It changed my life," or "It has had the greatest impact on my life of any ministry I have ever been involved with," or "It changed my whole perspective." I was overwhelmed!

I had been greatly blessed by the Walk Thru the Bible ministry over the years and was a long-time donor to them, but I found the situation to be a little awkward. Here I was at their big donor event, and people were praising FCCI and reminiscing about their past involvement with us. I wanted to make sure that I honored Walk Thru the Bible and in no way detracted from their fundraising efforts, so I kept quiet and prayed that God would bless their efforts. It was actually a good situation, showing me how God ministered to His people in different organizations in multiple ways. In a real sense, it was the working of the body of Christ.

I realized that God was revealing new truth to me. It was becoming clear to me that people who were no longer active in FCCI still had a deep love and appreciation for the ministry.

It begged the question of why they were no longer giving to the ministry or involved in it? The answer shocked me. It was because we had not asked them. Their overwhelming comments absolutely confirmed they would like to be involved if given the chance. They had time, talent, and treasure to go along with experience and wisdom. Essentially, they were an army of mentors or legacy leaders waiting to be called to active duty. A comment that George Barna had made years before popped into my mind. He said the largest group of new business starts in America was not immigrants or women, but people in the age group from 65 to 90. These people had retired or sold their businesses and wanted a way to give back, and we had the perfect way to deploy them.

All I really wanted when we started FCC was for a seasoned warrior to teach me how to operate a company for Christ and walk with me along the way. Only we couldn't find the seasoned warriors, but now we had legacy leaders who had walked that journey for many years and were waiting for their call to active duty. What an incredible thought to include a legacy leader in our Business Leadership Groups to bring additional wisdom and counsel, and possibly to help lead groups.

Legacy leaders are good soldiers, waiting for their next assignment across America and around the world.

KEY CONCEPTS

- Life change occurs in small groups. Are you in one? It's where you can get *advice without agenda*.

- God has a plan that includes you. Do you know what it is?

- God has to strip us of our pride if we are going to build a company for Him.

- We often start out in one direction, "knowing beforehand" what God is going to tell us, only to find out He's changed our direction and taught us an unexpected God-size truth.

- God speaks to us in a still, small voice. *Are you listening?*

JIM WHITE
The Power of Small Groups

Jim White is the owner of a CPA firm in Portland, Oregon. He became involved with FCCI in much the same way many of the people mentioned in this book did. He was invited to join a group by a man (Keith Gibson, in his case) who wanted to conduct his business with biblical principles. They met in his office every week for many years, and eventually they discovered FCCI and the resources they provide, and the group grew from there. They hired someone to help them grow their small group into a larger body called a "city team," and eventually that leader went to join the FCCI staff. At that point, Jim and his group began using FCCI as their provider of structure and resources. He says it's been a "joyful and beneficial ride" for him to go on.

Small groups have been at the backbone of Jim's ministry. Business owners and leaders come for an hour and a half to study what Christ has to say about running a business. They have two rules: Whatever gets said in here stays in here and no solicitation with one another. They try to maintain a policy of,"If I want your services, I'll come to you" between their members. Their original group has now split off a number of times so that there are as many as seventeen groups in the greater Portland-Vancouver area and even into various parts of the State of Oregon. They come together occasionally as a city team to learn what the others are doing and how they can support their community. One example of how they've done this is to take the *Crystal Darkness* documentary and message into the Portland area. Jim met with the chiefs of police and the sheriffs of the State of Oregon and distributed 200,000 booklets to these organizations to get them into the schools, and so on. There are many other examples of how they encourage one another by championing causes that their hearts and companies lead them to.

Christian business leadership has been a passion for Jim because, he says, "Initially, like most people, I became aware that my particular calling was to be a man of God, a great father and a great husband, but nobody ever taught me how to be a man. Nobody ever taught me to be a husband. Nobody ever taught me how to be a father. I saw examples of it from my parents ... a great family. The Promise Keepers was the first group environment that I was involved in that did a great job of teaching me how to be a man, father, and husband." Jim became involved with leading Promise Keepers small groups—eventually led more than 25 groups at his church. So the step into leading FCCI small groups was a natural one for him to take.

FCCI, through its annual conferences and video curriculum, began to teach him that many of the biblical principles of life—that the Lord has equipped us all uniquely, that we are to be in fellowship with one another (both in church and business), that our principle purpose is to live out our lives in such a way that God is given the glory, and that He uses us with our gifts and talents right where He placed us. In Jim's case, it was business, and he says, "It is my job to be a priest in the marketplace. The Lord has placed on each one of us that we are individually equipped to be a priest or the minister in the marketplace right where he placed us."

FCCI

CHAPTER 9

HISTORY, STRUCTURE, AND STRATEGY

*They devoted themselves to
the apostles' teaching and to fellowship,
to the breaking of bread and to prayer.*

ACTS 2:42 NIV

Two thoughts came together and had a profound impact on all ministry in the marketplace. One thought originated with a man who had been an atheist, and the other with a pastor in a small midwestern town.

When Larry Burkett was an atheist, he tried diligently to disprove God's Word. Instead, he came to a place where he recognized that God owns it all, we are stewards of what He has entrusted to us, and we must use what He has entrusted to us for His glory, not ours.

Charles Sheldon was a pastor in Topeka, Kansas, in 1896 and wrote *In His Steps*, which became one of the greatest, best-selling books of all time. He wrote about men and women receiving God's power when they faced every issue in life by asking, "What would Jesus do?" and then acting accordingly. These two thoughts came from very different perspectives, but they were the seed thoughts that germinated and grew into the Fellowship of Companies for Christ International. They were revolutionary thoughts in 1976, but they are still fresh and relevant today.

When God has placed us in an ownership or leadership position in a company, we need to understand that it is God's company and we must manage it in such a way as to honor Him. It is a very simple truth that is extremely difficult to grasp. As a matter of fact, it is almost impossible to grasp unless you have been called by God and are seeking to make your life count. In the early days, when we would share the story of FCC with fellow Christians, we would almost always receive a positive response. But only about 20 percent would move to take any action. And of the ones who were moved to action, only about 20 percent of those would go deep. Our experience says that only four percent move from receiving the word to *depth*. It is not a shallow ministry or a cheap one. There is a cost. "If any man will come after me, let him deny himself, and take up his cross daily, and follow me" (Luke 9:23 KJV). It might cost every bit as much as it costs the missionary who faces the witch doctor with the poison darts, but in both cases, God supplies the "shield of faith, with which you will be able to quench all the fiery darts of the devil" (Ephesians 6:16 KJV, emphasis mine). And in both cases, it is worth the cost.

Much of the history of FCCI has been shared in the preceding chapters. It was started by a group of non-descript businessmen who were following God's call on their lives, while trying to learn how to operate a company for Christ. They had little money, no resources, no staff, and no experience.

It had virtually no chance to succeed, but it did. God must get the glory, because man certainly cannot take any credit. The ministry was launched as a conference ministry in 1980, and shortly thereafter, small groups and study materials were added to the foundation of prayer. God clarified the purpose by adding the purpose statement—to equip and encourage chief executive officers and business owners to operate their businesses and conduct their personal lives in accordance with biblical principles in pursuit of Christ's eternal objectives. Then we added the Affirmations, which were a statement of faith that set forth what we believed. God blessed us and it was rich and we all knew for a fact that God had authored all of these foundational principles.

We were a lively bunch and were passionate about hearing these principles straight from God. We argued about every jot and tittle, because we wanted to get it right. We had made the commitment that we would not move forward unless we had unity. Sometimes it seemed like we were a million miles apart, but ultimately God always brought us together. Just like the authors of Scripture, we felt like we were hearing directly from God and that what we were writing down was God breathed. It was a powerful moment. We were ready to grow and many changes were in store for us, but the foundation was laid.

In the very early days, we delivered value to our members through conferences, small groups, and materials. Now we're able to deliver even more value through technology—the Internet, Twitter, YouTube, and so on. We want to be cutting edge and highly efficient, but we don't ever want to cut out the fellowship that occurs one on one or in small groups. This is the way we deliver "products" to our "customers."

However, we know that as new devices and systems evolve, we will incorporate improvements to our offerings. But for now, conferences, small groups, materials, and technology delivery systems will be the primary way we interact with our members.

The early boards of directors (made up primarily of founders) didn't just roll up their sleeves, argue and fight, and receive divine revelation from God; they had wonderful times of fellowship and camaraderie. We loved to eat good food, tell jokes, and laugh. We just had a good time with each other. We worked hard, but we also had great times of play. Some of the best moments we ever had were at the board meetings at Bert and Shirley's lake house at Lake Martin. Over the years we expanded them from one or two days to three or four. Inevitably God spoke to us at these meetings, often in between our wrestling matches. Great memories still remain of Bert cooking his famous tenderloin or skiing around the lake to the point of exhaustion.

Many funny stories evolved from our time at the lake. One night we decided to play charades. All of us were taking our turns with much bantering and laughter in the Stumbergs' family room. Then we realized that Jim Moye and Jimmy Pursell were missing. All of a sudden, we heard their laughter coming from under a table, behind the sofa. Neither one of them wanted to get up in front of the crowd, so they both headed to their hiding spot from different ends of the table. They bumped, and that's when the laughter started. They were caught!

Boisterous laughter erupted and all of us have continued to laugh about this story for the past twenty-some-odd years. We had great fun and deep love for each other.

THE FCCI CORE

CEOs and business owners were the very core of the ministry. For many years we didn't allow anyone other than CEOs, business owners, and their spouses to attend. We believed our advertisement—that it is lonely at the top—and we wanted it to be a safe and secure place for conversations, sharing, counsel, and intimate relationships. But we gradually felt that if we were going to build companies, we needed to open our fellowship up to CFOs and other key leaders. Subsequently, we were down at the lake once again and getting ready to leave after a board meeting, when Jimmy Pursell put forth the idea of the "Young Execs." He had children working for him who might, one day, run his business. He wanted to be sure that they were trained in the ways of FCCI. So, we all set our bags down and met for another several hours as we developed this new concept. Young Execs had a separate conference on a less elaborate scale, guided by Walt Wiley specifically for the children of our members plus up-and-coming young leaders within our companies. It was well received and went on for a number of years before we merged it back into the main body of FCCI. Dan Cathy of Chick-fil-A was very involved in the leadership of Young Execs in the early days of his involvement with FCCI. He later made the comment, "The time I spent in that circle of men (the leadership of FCCI) had more influence on my business life, as a Christian, than anything else I've experienced."[14]

In 2003, we wrote a new strategic plan. Originally, the core of the purpose statement was to "equip and encourage

14. Dan Cathy comments at Colonial Baptist Church in Cary, NC, June 20, 2012

chief executive officers and business owners." Although the purpose statement evolved into a mission and vision statement and included company leaders, the CEO (or business owner) is still at the core. It's where it all started, it's our roots, it's the foundation. We minister to the CEO by using conferences, groups, materials, and now technology to enable him to run a company for Christ. That company then joins with other companies to lead people to Christ, grow them up in the Lord, and serve our fellow man (SSS). That's the simple plan. But FCCI is complex in the outworking of all the details.

BOOKENDS

It's helpful to diagram or at least get a mental picture of how it all works. If you draw a box in the middle of a page with the CEO in it, you're at the heart of the ministry, or what we've been calling "the core." We then added two bookends. On one side you have executive leaders. David Rae said that when he was president of Apple Computers Canada, he could have used 75 percent of our materials if we, FCCI, had been open to him. We felt like God was screaming at us to fix that problem, so we added the executive leader category and included the Young Execs as well. The other bookend was Legacy Leaders. As people retired or sold their businesses, we wanted to retain our linkage with them. We wanted to leverage their time, talent, and treasure and build an army of coaches and mentors. So now we have three boxes—the CEO in the middle, and Executive Leaders and Legacy Leaders on either side.

We continued to feel God's leading as we modified the plan, but we realized that there were two more major steps that He was asking us to add. Outer bookends, if you would.

Continuing the thought of the diagram, one of these outer boxes contained pastors. Pastors are shepherds of the sheep, but there are also some "horses" and most pastors don't know how to deal with horses. Obviously, these "horses" are businessmen, and there is a barrier between pastors and businessmen in most churches! The only place they meet is at the budget meeting. As FCCI has noticed this in recent years, we have worked with pastors all over the world to help them better deal with their businessmen members, and we've equipped and encouraged businessmen to know that God owns it all and that they are just stewards of what he has entrusted them with. Kent Humphreys wrote *Shepherding Horses*, a book that has been widely used with great success in many countries to help pastors and their key laity. FCCI is uniquely positioned to help grow businessmen through proven techniques with over thirty years of materials in Bible study formats and leadership guides for group dynamics. It is a partnership between FCCI and the churches where we perfect or mature these businessmen for the work of the ministry (Ephesians 4:12 KJV), which is the biblical purpose of the church.

The other outer bookend is schools. We have worked with a number of schools over the past few years to provide materials for courses in business curriculums to expose their students to the concept of running a business as a platform for ministry and how to honor the Lord through that business. It is every bit as revolutionary to these young people as it was to us nearly forty years ago. It certainly gives these students a head start on this journey. John Duncan, the dean of the business school at Charleston Southern, started an FCCI

small group for students where they participated in a group modeled after FCCI's Business Leadership Groups, only at a greatly reduced cost, which was approximately the cost of textbooks! Hopefully, we're building integrity into these students, where faith and work come together and there is no compartmentalization.

Even more recently, we've started working with several seminaries. Pastors know very little about running a business, and the students who come out of the seminaries have continued that tradition. In many seminaries, secular business teachers are used to instruct these future church leaders. How much better is it for them to be taught by men and women who have walked out their faith in the marketplace and have a Christian worldview? They need to learn, like Ron O'Guinn, that pastors need the FCCI arrow in their quiver to use with their businessmen from time to time.

FCCI is all about fellowship, equipping, encouraging, prayer, standing on the foundation of God's Word, and pursuing Christ's eternal objectives. It is not about building monuments or turf, but building the kingdom of God. As I addressed in the discussion on naming the Fellowship of Companies for Christ, organizations cannot accept Christ. But in a very real way, FCCI is a steward of what God has entrusted to it! It means that it has pure motives and seeks to work with others, inside and outside the ministry, to glorify God by the bearing of much fruit. Partnerships, either formal or informal, allow us to join with others in a synergistic way to accomplish multiplied results. It is essential that these are perfectly aligned. If they are even slightly misaligned, the results will quickly become additive or evaporate altogether.

Most ministries today have a tendency to build turf. If they do, it is an absolute guarantee of misalignment and God's purposes will not be accomplished. Openhandedness and purity of motive along with blessing and guidance from God are essential. If the seminary students are to be blessed with a knowledge and respect of marketplace ministry, there must be alignment between the seminary and FCCI. All of this is the working of the body of Christ, where each of us has our particular role.

So, back to our diagram. The CEO/business owner is at the core, flanked by Executive Leaders and Legacy Leaders on either side, with the outer bookends being schools (business schools and seminaries) and pastors. Conferences, groups, materials, and technology are the primary tools used to equip and encourage along with mentoring, discipling, and counseling in our relationships utilizing partnerships with others to advance the game. What an unbelievably exciting call to walk out this vision.

FUNDING

We can't complete the story on the history, structure, and strategy of the ministry without a look at funding and finance. When we started FCC, we didn't give much thought to how we would pay for everything. We just knew that God had called, and we obeyed. But very early in the process, we came face to face with the funding issue. Initially, a few of us threw a few bucks into the pot and that sufficed, but as we moved into a three-day conference format at a resort with speakers, musicians, food, lodging, no staff, and materials, we realized we needed a plan and a budget. So, being business guys, we

put it together and decided that we were a donation-based ministry, with recommended giving levels based on company size. Everyone had to give if they wanted to be a member, but they could determine their own level. We had minimal costs that we watched very closely as we started to expand. There were two foundational principles of finance that we established early on. We would not be a begging ministry, and we would operate on the funds that God supplied. We would present an annual operating plan to our members and run the ministry on what we received. We made the decision that we would never borrow. If God didn't provide the money, we would assume that He didn't want us to do whatever it is we were planning to use the money for. This was the way we operated for many years, until we decided to charge dues and allow people to make contributions as God led them. We've had ups and downs, but we have walked along this path for nearly forty years, and God has supplied every step of the way.

In the early days, Larry Burkett was on the FCCI Board, and I was on the Christian Financial Concepts (CFC) Board. We were great friends and spent a lot of time together. One day Larry called me and asked me to come over to his office, which I did. When I arrived, Larry was in a somber mood. Money was just not coming in to CFC. We looked at the financial statements in detail, and it looked bleak. We prayed and wrung our hands. Finally, Larry said, "We're going to shut it down."

I responded by asking what he was talking about.

He said, "When I started CFC, I made a commitment to God that if He didn't supply the money, I would shut down the ministry. And that's what I'm going to do."

I was stunned. Rarely in my life had I ever seen a man
or a moment of such integrity. We talked on, and I urged
Larry to pray about it for a few more days, and he agreed. It
was not long before he got a call from the post office saying
they had a bunch of mail for CFC. He had recently changed
his mailing address, and the post office didn't know where
to deliver it. When they delivered the letters, the financial
problems went away and Larry actually had more money
than he needed. It was a test. God wanted to see if Larry
was holding the ministry with an open hand or not. Like
Abraham several thousand years before, Larry passed the test.
FCCI has always tried to operate with the same integrity that
Larry modeled to us so long ago.

KEY CONCEPTS

- There is a cost to going deep with the Lord,
  but it is worth the cost.

- "All things are possible to him that believeth"
  (Mark 9:23). Have you trusted Him to do the
  impossible? If not, why not?

- How has God called you? Did you obey? Are
  there any regrets?

- What do you love most? Are you willing to
  sacrifice it to honor God? Do you trust Him
  enough to lay it on the altar?

BILL LEONARD
The Foundation of FCCI

Bill Leonard, president of Wm. Leonard & Co., a real estate consulting firm based in Atlanta that focuses on serving technology companies, grew up with Bobby Mitchell; they were best friends in high school. In 1976, Bobby and his wife, Sue, began witnessing to Bill and his wife, Sandy, who was already a believer, inviting them to attend Bible studies and church with them. And finally, after about six months of fellowship, heart-to-heart talks, and close friendship, Bill committed his life to serving Christ. So, when Bobby became interested in studying what Scripture had to say about running a business, he, of course, called his old friend Bill.

"FCCI has had a greater impact on me spiritually than any organization over the last thirty-seven years," Bill says. "We were pioneering "marketplace ministry" in those days. No one else was talking about it. But we knew God wanted to use our businesses as a platform for ministry, as a tool or vehicle to reach people for Jesus Christ."

It started with the externals. "When you become a Christian you start going to church, reading your bible and praying. Doing those things you're supposed to do, working on the checklist," said Bill. "So we started looking for ways to make our company 'Christian.' You know, put a cross or ichthus in our logos. We've got to be visible about this, right? 'I'm not ashamed of the gospel.' We've got to put a Bible out in the reception area and have a Bible study in our office. These are the kinds of things we thought that we needed to do if we're going to be a Christian company. So we worked on the externals, but God began to show us it's not about those externals as much as it is really about the internals. It was really about the change in our hearts."

So God began to move them from the externals to the internals as He really dealt with their lives. Nevertheless, they did lots of external things in their business as well. Bill did put the ichthys in his logo. And where most companies send out Christmas cards, Bill's sent out Easter cards. "You only received one Easter card and it made an impact. We were a small business, but we sent out thirty-five hundred Easter cards every year for five to six years. It was about a $5,000 per year investment, but it was a way of expressing our faith in the marketplace. We got some nice compliments . . . and a few of them came back telling us to keep our religion out of our business. But they were done in good taste and professionally designed. Years later I was in a competitor's office and he showed me where he had all of our Easter cards displayed on his bookshelf. Only in heaven will we know the full impact of our lives here on earth."

Then, in 1989 God opened the door to the technology community in Atlanta for Wm. Leonard & Co and they began to focus all of their marketing efforts on technology companies, which were booming. In 1992, the company became a sponsor of High Tech Month, which was a focus on technology for the month of October every year. As a sponsor, they had the right to host an event under the umbrella of High Tech Month to leverage the marketing, and they were trying to figure out some type of event that would get some exposure for their company. That's when God gave Bill the idea to organize an evangelistic prayer breakfast for the technology community. "It was a big risk but I knew it was from God and He would take care of us regardless of how it was received. It turned out to be the most rewarding thing we have ever done in business."

They recruited host committee members to buy a table for ten, and invite their non-Christian friends in technology to join them. They had a high-profile speaker who shared his or her faith story and gave people an opportunity to make a decision for Jesus Christ. That first year there were seventeen host committee members and about three hundred fifty guests. People's lives were changed as they gave their lives to Christ. The host committee members followed up with their guests and the breakfasts continued. In 1995, they formed High Tech Ministries, a non-profit organization, to direct the events of the ministry. In 2013, they will have their 22nd Annual High Tech Prayer Breakfast with sixteen hundred guests. In fact, for the last fifteen years, it's been the largest event in the technology community each year with as many as two thousand in attendance at the height of the tech boom.

They've also added about fifteen Bible studies called Grace@ Work groups that meet weekly throughout the technology community led by business men and women. Everything is done in a business environment because, "If you're not a believer and I want to invite you to my church, regardless of the denomination . . . that's a barrier. Many people have had bad experiences in church or they are unchurched and don't feel comfortable in a strange environment. We invite them into a business environment they are familiar with so there are fewer obstacles. Our bottom line is changed lives.

Our mission is to lead people in the Atlanta Technology community into a life-changing relationship with Jesus Christ by creating business environments where God can be discovered." They also started a service initiative called Serve@Work where believers in technology can invite their non-Christian associates to join them in a service project in the inner city. It is a great bonding experience, breaks down barriers and opens the door to an evangelistic opportunity through the prayer breakfast or another event. It is all based on relationship evangelism . . . earning the trust of fellow workers by investing in their lives, caring about their needs and then inviting them to join you to hear the gospel.

It's been incredible how these prayer breakfasts have been received. In fact, the breakfast was featured on the front page of the Southeast Edition of the *Wall Street Journal* in 1998. This all came out of FCCI, the idea of using a business as a platform for ministry. They recruit speakers who are well-known business executives, preferably in technology, to help draw guests to the breakfast. "We invite them into our world on *their* terms," Bill explains, "We describe it as the earliest networking event on the planet starting at 5:59 A.M., but we are careful to also let our guests know it is an evangelistic event." In 2008 the ministry started the Ambassadors Leadership program, a mentoring program to train the next generation of leaders in the ministry, and this year 125 men and women will have completed the program.

In addition, they helped ten other groups start their own industry-specific prayer breakfasts, six in Atlanta and four out-of-state duplicating the High Tech Prayer Breakfast model. The Commercial Real Estate Prayer Breakfast in Atlanta recently completed their fifteenth annual prayer breakfast and the DC Metro High Tech Prayer breakfast is preparing for its eleventh annual event this year. "Having a prayer breakfast in both the commercial real estate and technology industries has allowed me to totally integrate my business and my ministry so that it is easy to raise the topic of faith with most everyone I talk to on a daily basis," adds Bill.

"The vision God gave me twenty-two years ago is that one day when people look at the technology community in Atlanta, Georgia, the differentiator, the thing that will set us apart from any other technology community is the light of Jesus Christ shining out from our community. And we believe God is bringing that about in His timing. But that's all a result of the vision that God gave Bobby through the Fellowship of Companies for Christ."

FCCI

CHAPTER 10

FUTURE VISION AND THE NEXT GENERATION

We will tell the next generation
the praiseworthy deeds of the Lord, his power,
and the wonders he has done.

PSALM 78:4 NIV

The foundation is well laid. Many of the principles are timeless. God owned it all yesterday and He will still own it all tomorrow. He never changes. "Jesus Christ the same yesterday, and today, and forever" (Hebrews 13:8 KJV).

But we change. We're born into this world, we grow and mature physically, and we ultimately die. That is true for every one of us. Somewhere along life's journey, if we believe in Jesus Christ and accept His gift of salvation, we are born again and will have everlasting life; if we don't believe, we will not have life. In this world, we can only be one of God's stewards if we believe and become Christians. Then God can use us and trust us to manage some of His assets. If we happen to be business owners or company leaders with the authority to commit the company to Him, then I believe that

God entrusts us with the responsibility to run that company for Christ. It's a call that most don't hear, but it's rich beyond measure for those who do. Some hear it and just ignore it because it's difficult and requires courage and faith, but it is a path that pleases God if we choose to take it. Many think the Great Commission might well be completed in and through the marketplace. We've been discussing how to do that throughout this book, but now we're looking at where do we go from here and how do we *pass it on*.

In the formative days, we had no staff, no money, and no resources. We did have a clear vision. We, as primarily small company owners, wanted to operate a company on biblical principles. The foundation of this vision was based on the thought that God owns it all and we are stewards of what he entrusted us with. The guiding question is, "What would Jesus do?" We named the ministry the Fellowship of Companies for Christ, with a focus on fellowship, but without the I. We also developed a statement of faith called the affirmations, and we continued fleshing out conferences, groups, and materials. There were a million other details and we answered them as we could, but this was the essence of what we started with, and this initial vision was clear to everyone involved. The reality of it all was that we were trying diligently to operate our own companies as platforms for ministry. Most of us were still at the stage of trying to give our companies to God and finding that we continued to take them back with some regularity, only to give them to Him again and repeat the cycle. We were not focused on the Great Commission.

Other changes followed, including adding the I to our

name and writing several strategic plans. We added the *I* for *international* in 1990, but it was more than ten years later before it had any real impact. In our strategic plans, we sought to expand the ministry and make it more accessible next door and around the world. We changed logos, shifted the purpose statement to mission and vision statements, and invited company leaders as well as CEOs and business owners. Many changes occurred, but the initial vision remained in tact as our foundation. Now, we stand looking into the future at transforming communities and completing the Great Commission. We've gone from trying to "fix my company" to completing the great task that God has given to the human race. To say that this is an expansion of the vision is a gross understatement.

When you ask about the next generation and the future vision of FCCI, you need to know our current vision, where we've come from, and where we're going. The parable of the cloth and the wineskins gives us some insight. "No one puts a piece of unshrunk cloth on an old garment; for the patch pulls away from the garment, and the tear is made worse. Nor do they put new wine into old wineskins, or else the wineskins break, the wine is spilled, and the wineskins are ruined. But they put new wine into new wineskins, and both are preserved (Matthew 9:16–17 NKJV)." This expansion of the vision requires us to deepen our hearts to become larger than companies. We must have new wineskins.

As we said, the foundation is well laid and there are many timeless principles. *The call to use companies as platforms for ministry in the marketplace is as strong today as it's ever been.* It remains a compelling vision, but times are changing in America and around the world. Technology has ushered in a rapidly changing environment and many new opportunities that were unthinkable only a few years ago.

People change as well. The baby boomers are entering their retirement years, and the millennials are now making an impact on the workforce. The X and Y generations are in between, and none of these groups process the same way. Communication has always been difficult but never moreso than now; you will not be able to communicate with each of these groups in the same way with the same effectiveness. One is not better than the other; they are just different. FCCI will have to be sensitive to the needs of each group and tailor programs and materials accordingly, but we must let these horses run. There is a tenuous balance between the old and the new, but they both rest on a solid foundation.

We must keep the foundational treasures of yesterday and build on them with the good things of today and tomorrow. The issue quickly becomes, What is good? In Genesis, God said, "It is *good*!" as He created the world. We know from the book of James (1:17) that every *good* and perfect gift comes from above, and we know from Paul's letter to the Ephesians (2:10) that God prepared *good* works for us before we were even born, that we might walk in them. Psalm 133:1 says, "Behold, how *good* and pleasant it is for brethren to dwell together in unity!" (NKJV). In Scripture we find many references to good, but if we're going to apply "good things"—such as new techniques, technology, and ways of processing to our foundation—they must be scrutinized through a biblical prism and added by a committed hand. The Church at Berea is a good model for us to follow. Paul describes them as *more noble* than the church at

Thessalonica because "they received the word with all readiness of mind, and searched the scriptures daily, whether those things were so" (Acts 17:11 KJV).

The wineskin of FCCI must be able to hold the new wine. Old wineskins would already be stretched to their limit. New wine would expand over time and burst the old skin. The new wine must include a deepening of the heart to become larger than the company! "What would Jesus do?" was a very simple statement that birthed a call—a revolutionary way to look at business. Out of the Atlanta marketplace, the Lord, through a few men, birthed *marketplace ministry*. FCCI started local, we planted local, but God called us to be global. The Great Commission itself calls us to the ends of the earth. The vision of FCCI has always been a big vision, a global vision, and a relevant vision because it is a vision based on Christ's eternal objectives.

Today, FCCI's mission and vision have not changed but have been refreshed, renewed, and revitalized in big, global, and relevant ways that the founders and other builders of FCCI could not complete in just one lifetime. It's now time to pass the baton to others for the next level of God's call.

Who are we? Where are we going? What is our future vision? FCCI is one ministry. It used to be one ministry in name only, with a number of compartmentalizing silos, but now it is one unified Global ministry. It is our purpose to equip and encourage *all* Christian CEOs, business owners, and their company leaders, wherever they are, with the very best materials available. It is not based on age, race, or gender. If you run a company, we want to help you honor Christ on your journey and produce kingdom fruit. We then want to link you with leaders of other companies to transform the world and ultimately to complete the Great Commission. Each company and each leader may have a different call, but we are to function together as the body of Christ to accomplish God's purposes. Our roles will change as we go down this road, but we can all contribute at every stage.

Paul wrote to Timothy advising him how to build and grow churches. Much of what he wrote could be applied to a business context, particularly an FCCI context, where a senior guy in his latter days is pouring wisdom into an emerging leader. He wrote, "Let no one despise your youth, but be an example to the believers in word, in conduct, in love, in spirit, in faith, in purity" (1 Tim. 4:12 NKJV). Henry Blackaby said, "When God chooses a spiritual leader, character, *not age*, is the determining factor."[15] Godly people need evidence of a relationship with God in their leaders before they will follow.

I asked one of my sons for his advice on how to reach the younger folks. He said, "Dad, you're still on target with the focus on the marketplace, but you need to work on communication with them. *Depth is key!* The middle ground in America is going away. There is only a small sliver of millenials and the Y generation who are committed enough to hear this call. Recently a man made the statement to me that, "There are no Christian young people in America." He followed that with the question, "Right?" I responded by saying, "No, and a thousand times no! There might be only a sliver of young people, but they are highly committed and seeking to change the world. They actually want to hear the message of FCCI and want to accelerate it." He

15. Note on 1 Timothy 4:12, Blackaby Study Bible.

went on to describe a recent event at his church where they attracted 60,000 young people for several days of meetings in downtown Atlanta. They were focused on worship and service and stopping the sex trade. The event was organized and directed by young leaders. It was a great success. Never had he seen so many young people work so hard and be so committed. He noticed that they often sat around tables of six, working feverishly on their laptops, but no one talked. The good news is that we have a sliver to reach and teach, but we must learn how to communicate with them.

Many young people have started businesses, conceived of great ideas, or even been strong leaders at very young ages. I started my first business when I was ten years old. My father was a college professor in Ceramic Engineering, and he gave me a small hobby kiln for Christmas. He gave me instructions on how to use it and a few business principles to boot.

I enlisted my buddy next door to help. It wasn't long before we were putting enamel coatings on copper disks; soldering ear bobs or cuff links on the back; and selling earrings, cuff links, and pins to every teacher, neighbor, relative, or bystander we could find. We were very prosperous. My dad was helping us, but he required that we cover all our own expenses and operate within our means. At the time, we were paying a nickel for a copper disk, which was about the size of a penny. I wanted to reduce our costs, so I wrote the Department of the Treasury asking for permission to use pennies instead of buying copper disks. Shockingly, I got a return letter. It said that although they could not approve of defacing money, they didn't think it would be a problem in the volumes I was dealing with. So we immediately shifted to pennies with our quasi approval to do so. The business didn't last much longer, but my relationship with my buddy did. We have been involved in a number of business ventures over the past fifty years, and we've never had even one cross word. The lessons of fairness, honesty, and integrity that my dad taught us have followed us all the days of our lives.

Many of the stories shared in this book involve young people. Horst Schulze started working in the hotel industry as a busboy at the age of fifteen and coined the motto that followed him for the rest of his career: "Ladies and Gentlemen Serving Ladies and Gentlemen." I was twenty-seven years old when God started wrestling with me over my integrity and His call on my life to the marketplace. I never wanted to start a ministry; I just wanted a mentor to disciple me and teach me how to operate a company as a platform for ministry. I tried to find one, but there was no one to do it, so even though I was young and inexperienced, I answered God's call with the other founders and started FCCI. In Scripture, David slew Goliath and Mary gave birth to Jesus as teenagers. Michelangelo sculpted La Pieta at twenty-five. Great things have been accomplished by youth throughout the centuries.

Even as we draw close to the finish line, we can still accomplish great things for God. Caleb wholeheartedly followed the Lord through the difficulties of the wilderness, and he cried out as they entered the Promised Land when he was eighty-five, to "give me this mountain!"[16] He wanted to fight the giants. In 2006 at the International Conference in Pasadena, Bert Stumberg, at eighty-three, was recruiting Legacy Leaders to sign up and go! Kent Humphreys had 20 percent breathing

16. Joshua 14:12

capacity the last few years of his life, but he continued to travel internationally, speaking to thousands of people and writing several books. Ralph Meloon and Stanley Tam are still productive for the Lord at ninety-four and ninety-seven respectively. All of these men and many, many others have finished or are finishing strong, running across the finish line. They have been intentional about making their lives count. "Those who are planted in the house of the Lord / Shall flourish in the courts of our God. / They shall still bear fruit in old age; / They shall be fresh and flourishing" (Ps. 92:13–14 NKJV). Clearly, age is not a factor in God's economy!

I believe we are called at this time and to this platform to be ministering to a world spinning out of control! We see it all around us; immorality is always preceded by impiety. We know that the heart of a person is flawed before the immoral act. Corruption has now outpaced poverty as the world's most concerning issue. Corruption and all that goes with it—lack of integrity, greed, power abuse, and bribery. We are dealing with a nation (and a world) where irrationality is becoming more and more prevalent. *Truth* is slowly being removed from our thinking and society; it is being educated out of our youth. When truth leaves nations, they are totally destroyed and decimated.

FCCI offers the experience of ministering to a nation through business. FCCI is a community of business leaders united by a vision that Christ can change our world through how we do business. This is the call that God has placed on us. What if we could provide answers to the world's questions about biblical principles in the workplace, turn the world's unemployment to employment, and bring hope into at-risk communities by changing their economies? What if we could care for our employees better than the government or any secular companies? It is our vision that our world is transformed through one company leader at a time. Thousands of men and women called to make a difference. Here are some more what-ifs:

- What if one percent of Christian business leaders from around the world were to join the FCCI movement? Would our world be different? Would our communities be different?

- What if the strongest business leaders in the world were affiliated with or were members of FCCI—what would happen?

- What if FCCI would be a model of corporate unity and excellence?

- What *will* happen when business leaders care more about integrating a biblical worldview into the workplace where the focus is on mission and service versus materialism and money?

This type of cultural shift is change, real change. It sounds far-reaching, but with God all things are possible! This ministry can change the world, but it can also change the heart of the man or woman next door. Sometimes we know about it, sometimes we don't. I didn't know that Robert Shaw had been impacted for Christ in the Bible study that I taught at the plant until ten years later. But, remember this truth—any assignment from God, regardless of whether we think it's big or small, is a God-size assignment and is important to the King.

Recently, one of our FCCI members sent in a letter written by a thirteen-year-old son of an employee. It touched his heart and it touched mine. This is the kind of shift, the kind of heart change that can take down strongholds and transform lives. Our FCCI member wrote, "I'm sharing this so that it might encourage others to get a vision for the depth of impact they can have on people God has brought into their sphere of influence. It is likely that a 'touch' of this magnitude would have never happened without the equipping and encouraging of FCCI."

Here's an excerpt from the letter the thirteen-year-old wrote to our business owner:

Ever since I can remember, my father mentioned working for a great company, owned by an equally kind man. He often tells my siblings and me that the reason we are blessed with a warm, comforting home and enough food to eat is because of you.

I wanted to personally thank you on behalf of the entire family for giving my father work and supplying my family with the money to live the life we have. Even though we've never met, I'd like to thank you and your wife for being a part of our lives, and for all that you give to my father, who in turn gives to his family. All the blessings we receive from you really do make a difference in our lives.

This is how lives are being transformed. Communities should never look the same when there are FCCI companies in the city. At FCCI, we are attempting something so bold and so great that it is doomed to fail unless God is in it. We have a big vision and a mission that can bring transformation. God is calling us to reach out at home and throughout the world to even more business leaders, embracing the next generation by equipping and encouraging them as they impact their sphere of influence for Christ. FCCI opens up the opportunity for the intervention of God. What an exciting journey! Come join us!

KEY CONCEPTS:

- Receive the Word with all readiness of mind and search Scripture daily to see if it is so.

- Deepen your heart to become larger than your company; work diligently to transform the world for Christ and complete the Great Commission.

- "Train up a child in the way he should go, and when he is old, he will not depart from it" (Prov. 22:6 KJV).

- Regardless of your age, race, or gender, be intentional to bear *much fruit* for the Lord.

HORST SCHULZE
Excellence in All Things

How did you start along your path of excellence?

I left my home when I was fourteen. My parents found me a job as a busboy about a hundred miles away from home. It was a very first-class hotel. Everybody in the family said, "This is such a fine hotel; we could never go there. You have to behave yourself; the guests are important," and so on. When we arrived there, the general manager talked to my mother and me and said, "Don't get envious. The guests are very important guests and we are just here to serve them." On Wednesdays I went to hotel school, and I worked as a busboy the rest of the week. After about a year and a half, our teacher in the hotel school said, "I would like you to now write an essay, three pages, about what you feel about your industry now." I was fifteen years old by this time, and I decided to write about a maître d' because everybody was saying the guests are the most important people, but the guests thought that the maître d' was. When he walked into the room, you knew he was there. There was an excellence about him; he never would have walked into a room without looking perfect. He went from one table to the next explaining things and recommending food and wine. He spoke English. He spoke French. He spoke German. And as a consequence for his excellence, he was the most respected person in the room by the guests, even though everybody said the guests are the most important. My essay was titled "We Are Ladies and Gentlemen Serving Ladies and Gentlemen." This became my hotel's motto. You don't go to work to work.

You go to work to be excellent in what you are doing. That stayed with me at a very impressionable time of my life. It's excellence that you pursue, no matter what you do. There is no good work for lazy people. There is always good work for excellent people.

How did you make that shift from Hilton and Hyatt to the Ritz Carlton?

I was working for Hyatt headquarters in Chicago as Operations Vice-President and somebody called me and said we're starting a new company. They needed an operator to run that new company. I had a great career and I liked Chicago, but he kept on calling. Then he made a comment to me saying, you can run the company your way. It's your company. I asked if I could establish all philosophies, all, and they said, "Sure you run this. Your company."

So I got intrigued. I started to dream about some of this. I had a vision of what I would do and that started to control me. I ended up accepting the job. It was a dream. I had a vision. We prayed on it unbelievably heavily , Sheri and I. And it was pretty clear to us that it was the thing to do. The first year and a half was disastrous. It was absolutely disastrous, and I didn't tell my wife. She had just had a baby. We had no house. We had debt. I didn't want to burden her with the job was not working out, but eventually I sat down with my wife and I said, "Honey, this may not work out. We may have made a mistake coming here." But what my wife said was very simple. "Why would you argue with God? We prayed on it very heavily. Maybe the job doesn't work out, but we still did the right thing coming here." Wow. Of course, that's history.

I left the company [Ritz-Carlton] eighteen years later and it was the most successful hotel company ever at that time. For a moment there, it didn't look right. But we kept on being driven by the vision of creating excellence. It's as simple as that. That's the vision. We will be respected as the best hotel company in every location where we are.

So now you're retired?
My family wanted me to retire because I traveled about two hundred days a year, long overseas trips, and so on. I retired on a Friday and spent the first weekend at home, and I looked back and realized I really could have done it better. All I could think of was, What are you going to do now? I asked one neighbor what would you do? Why did you retire? And he said, to do what I like to do, and I said, "Oh gosh, what do I like to do? I like to do hotels." So on Monday I looked for an office and told my wife I was going to start another hotel company [Capella Hotels]. She thought I was insane. She was negative about it for about a week, and then she said, "Hey, that's who you are. I'll support you. I'm with you and I stand with you," and that's what happened.

How did you get involved with FCCI?
I'm in a Bible class with Bobby Mitchell. I participated a few times in meetings. To me, supporting and getting together with people in business leadership and listening to the Word and getting guidance out of it, fellowshipping with them, learning from each other, and of course, listening to the Word ... I set out to deliberately try to keep God in the workplace. In my opinion, that's the key thing that can keep us as a country on track.

What would be the one take away that you would like to give readers of this book?

Well, you see companies hiring people to fulfill certain functions—in the hotel business it may be to hire somebody to cook food or to check people into the hotel. But if I run an organization of integrity, I hire people to join me in my dream. If we, as believers, know that our fellow man is loved by God, we will hire people to participate in our dream for our company. We start by saying we want to be the best in whatever industry we're in, then we talk about function later. So the takeaway as a Christian leader is you make sure you hire the best people to be part of your dream, including the dishwasher. That is what a great Christian organization has to offer.

Appendix A
FCCI CORE VALUES

- God is the Owner; we are stewards of His companies.
- The Bible is the ultimate authority for life and business.
- Prayer is the lifeblood of our relationship with the Owner.
- We are *called* to work/ministry. Living a fully integrated, balanced life is a biblical mandate.
- Integrity is a non-negotiable essential.
- Commitment to excellence is a hallmark of a Christian in business.
- Community is a key to walking with Christ.
- Being relevant to our time and culture is crucial to our impact.
- Focus on building. The kingdom of God takes priority over building any organization.

FCCI CORE PRINCIPLES

1. The priesthood of the believer—a special calling to serve God in and through his or her business and company.

2. There is no sacred/secular split in living out the Christian faith.

3. Eternal values take precedent over temporal values.

4. A Christian company is not necessarily better than a non-Christian company, but it must be different.

5. Christian CEOs are stewards, not owners.

FCCI'S STATEMENT OF FAITH ("THE AFFIRMATIONS")

LEADERSHIP
As a Company Leader...

I. I believe Jesus Christ is the Son of God and have personally accepted His gift of salvation.

II. I believe the Bible is God's inspired revelation to man and endeavor to live in obedience to its principles and commands.

III. I am a member in good standing of a local church and support the work of Christ through the church by my time, talents, and financial resources.

IV. I am a member in good standing of Fellowship of Companies for Christ International, supporting our Vision, Values, and Mission, leveraging my time, talent, treasure and relationships for the Kingdom.

CORPORATE
A Company Leader strives through
the company as his / her position allows ...

I. Sharing the Gospel of Jesus Christ with its
employees and also its customers, competitors,
suppliers, and other business contacts.

II. Taking an active part In the development of the
spiritual and Christian testimony of its employees.

III. Operating in accordance with the commands
and principles of Scripture In dealing with
its finances, in handling Its personnel, and in
administering its policies.

IV. Regularly giving or encouraging giving a portion
of its financial and personnel resources in meeting
various Christian responsibilities in accordance
with Scripture. This pertains to the needs of
its employeesas well as others, and may be
accomplished through direct gifts or through
contributions to agencies and ministries.

BIBLICAL
I. There is one God, eternally existing in three
persons: the Father, the Son, and the Holy Spirit.

II. The Bible Is God's written and inspired
revelation to man and Is the primary authority
for man's life.

III. The deity of Jesus Christ, His virgin birth,
sinless life, miracles, death on the cross to provide
salvation, resur(ectlon, and bodily ascension

into heaven, present ministry of intercession for us, and His return to earth in power and glory.

IV. The personality and deity of the Holy Spirit, His power to perform the miracle of new birth in unbelievers and to Indwell believers, enabling them to live a Godly life.

V. Man was created in the image of God and because of sin was alienated from God. That alienation can be removed only by accepting, through faith, God's gift of salvation which was made possible by Christ's atoning death and resurrection.

VI. Jesus Christ Is the Head of the Church, and all believers are to assemble together regularly for worship, for edification through the Scriptures, and for mutual encouragement.

VII. Jesus Christ commanded all believers to proclaim the Gospel throughout the world and to discipline men of every nation. The fulfillment of that Great Commission requires that all worldly and personal ambitions be subordinated to a total commitment to 'Him who loved us and gave Himself for us'.

CHRONOLOGY

1977—The founders form the first group (Christian Business Fellowship)

1980—FCC was launched at the first conference in downtown Atlanta at the Marriott Hotel

1980–1986—Bruce Wilkinson, Larry Burkett, and Ron Blue join the Fellowship casting vision and articulating the key teachings

1985–1989—Don Kline and Buck Jacobs and Mike Stevens become the first Area Coordinators and lead expansion

1989—FCC becomes FCCI, emphasizing the fellowship's international vision. Growth triggers restructuring. Board of Directors appoints Ray Miller as the first President and CEO to take over operations

1990–1996—Executive Team grows to include the first Vice-President, Doug Hunter, active for many years as a member and business owner. Area coordinators grow to twenty under the supervision of Don Kline

1996—A changing of the guard prompts the development of a new God-sized strategic plan.

Bert Stumberg retires as Chairmen, Bobby Mitchell takes his place, and Alan Ross comes on as the new CEO

Fall 1996—Largest ever International Conference challenges members to support new vision; changing our world through Christ one company at a time

1999—Growth exceeds 2,000 members in the U.S.

2001—FCCI merges with Crown Financial Ministries

2002–2008—Kent Humphreys steps into the role of CEO, bringing his dynamic leadership and powerful teaching to FCCI at a critical time. Under his leadership, FCCI, using the Christ@Work brand, expands internationally into several thousand members in over 30 countries. God moves leaders to expand the mission to serve business leaders—owners, executives, entrepreneurs, professionals and business students. Vision recast as transforming the world through Christ, one business leader at a time

2008—Doug Hunter returns as CEO with a heart to inspire business leaders everywhere for maximum kingdom impact and global transformation

2010—Our emphasis in the USA is on new groups in every state, bringing the ministry of FCCI closer to every Christian CEO

2011—Terence Chatmon is unanimously appointed President & CEO, bringing a heart for discipleship and a passion for encouraging and equipping business leaders to further the kingdom, September. Global Cities Plan is launched, targeting the top one hundred strategic cities–worldwide.

2012—New York City Area Team launches, April 2-3, 2012. Terence Chatmon announces new technology advances, including the 2012 launch of FCCI's first Global Learning Portal and Conference Streaming event. Global Cities Plan announced.

As we look to the future, we see an unprecedented opportunity to unite business leaders worldwide, and see Christ honored in the workplace as never before.

ACKNOWLEDGEMENTS

The writing of this book has been a journey. I have written it by recording interviews, riding on planes, bumping down roads, trying to get connected in China and in my study at home. For the most part, I'm sharing stories of the journey I've been on for the past 40 years. It's sort of fun to remember the good times and reminisce. My travels have taken me to more than 60 countries and around the world several times, but more importantly they have connected me to unique friends who have blessed me richly. They have been the joy of my life. I consider myself the most blessed man in the world. It's been awesome and amazing. Truly an abundant life.

My wife has been my helpmate, and the mother of my children. She's been with me every step of the way. She's supported me, encouraged me, cried with me, and laughed with me. She's also been part of FCCI from the very first moment. It's core to her life. She has helped me write this book, but she might well have told an even more compelling story. She's the light of my life. Thank you and God bless you!

I hired Terence to be the President of FCCI, and he has been a joy and a blessing. But in regards to this book he has been the initiator and the prodder and the gentle pusher that has gotten me to write it. Thank you. He's also put me with a great writer in Kate Etue and a wonderful publisher always think of Kent as a warrior, ready to preach a sermon or make a friend at a moments notice. He and his wife Davidene have been wonderful friends and writers of the FCCI Gospel. Smith Lanier and Jimmy Pursell were early Board members, and Cade Willis opened Asia for FCCI.

The book is a book of stories. Some mine, but many from others. Thanks for all of the testimonies, comments and illustrations that make this book work. My dear friend Henry Blackaby constantly reminds me not to ask God to bless my good plans, but to ask God how I can serve him. Stanley Tam at 97 and Ralph Meloon at 95 continue to be inspirations of how to run the race. Marian Noronha (slaves), John Coors (Kenya), and Hortz Schultz (excellence) show us how to get out of the box. David Rae, Terry Parker and Tom Hill all shared inputs on how to extend the impact of a company's ministry outside of the corporate walls. Jim White and Ted Sprague have had great impact in our group ministry and have been leaders in building men. Thanks to Bill Moeny for his leadership in our prayer ministry, which is the unspoken power that undergirds FCCI.

Thanks to the past, current, and future Board members who have all contributed so generously of their time, talent and treasure, in addition to our staff, led by Frank Vann, and our group, area, and international leaders. Thanks also to the army of volunteers who contribute more that 120,000 hours annually.

Thanks to all with love and blessings,
Bobby Mitchell

in Derrick Miles of Milestone. This team has been patient, kind, understanding, and diligent. Thanks is just not a big enough word.

I would also like to thank all of the people involved with the founding of FCCI. It would not have existed without Bert Stumberg. He was our first Chairman and a wise, experienced business man who guided the rest of us along the way. Bill Leonard is probably my closest friend, who has been a great encouragement and motivator to me. I watched him turn from the all opponents team to being a giant in the Christian community. Jim Moye was an uninvited guest at our first gathering of men, but God handled the invitation list, so he has been a stalwart in FCCI ever since. Ben Lively was the first guy I ever called to test the thought of FCCI, and he responded instantaneously without even the slightest hesitation and has been a faithful steward on our journey. Thomas Harris was my quiet steady prayer partner who was so very consistent. And finally, Larry Burkett was my great friend and mentor who gently pushed me to embrace my call to the marketplace. He poured God's wisdom into my life and taught me that when we're shaken, what we've got inside comes out. Special thanks to the wives of the founders, who caught the vision early and helped us see the critical need for the spouse to understand the call equally as much as the CEO.

It's hard to name all the people who have impacted my life, and created these stories, but several have to be mentioned. Bruce Wilkinson is another friend and mentor. Along with Larry Burkett, he was the major builder of the FCCI doctrine and teacher of our members. Thank you!

Kent Humphreys was another giant in the FCCI world. I'll